SIMPLY SWISS

**64 ESSENTIAL RECIPES
FROM THE HEART OF EUROPE**

To my fellow Swiss-food fans—cheese connoisseurs, fondue fanatics, raclette enthusiasts, *Birchermüesli* devotees, *Zopf* lovers, chocolate fanciers—and anyone who's Swiss-food curious, this book's for you.

Simply Swiss
64 essential recipes from the heart of Europe

Text and photography: © Andie Pilot
Additional photography: Samuel Bucheli
Illustrations, cover design, typesetting and layout: Ajša Zdravković
Editors: Aude Pidoux and Angela Wade
Proofreader: Karin Waldhauser

ISBN: 978-3-03964-079-9
First edition: 2025
Deposit copy in Switzerland: 2025
Printed in the Czech Republic

© 2025 HELVETIQ SA
Mittlere Strasse 4
4056 Basel
Switzerland

HELVETIQ
helvetiq.com

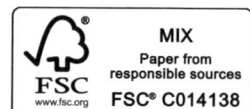

FSC
www.fsc.org

MIX
Paper from
responsible sources
FSC® C014138

ANDIE PILOT

SIMPLY SWISS

64 ESSENTIAL RECIPES FROM THE HEART OF EUROPE

TABLE OF CONTENTS

SOUPS 18

GLORIOUS CHEESE 34

SIDES 48

MAINS 58

APÉRO 84

BOUNTIFUL BREAD 92

WHAT'S INSIDE?

This book is full of Switzerland's best—and best-known—recipes. From buttery braided *Zopf* to creamy *Birchermüesli*, this book contains all the Swiss culinary classics, as well as plenty of regional dishes (*Capuns*! *Cholermüs*! *Cuchaule*! *Chäshörnli*!) from all corners of the country.

But what's so great about Swiss food anyway?

Swiss cuisine is a balancing act.

Sometimes the simplest raw ingredients are processed by cutting-edge technology; like pure Swiss milk in state-of-the-art cheese or chocolate factories. The culinary influences from neighboring France, Germany, Italy, and Austria are seamlessly incorporated; for example, when dried pasta made it over the border, alpine herdsmen quickly began to bring this light, energy-dense foodstuff with them into the Alps, then used their abundant supply of milk and cheese to make their famous dish, *Älplermagronen*. They serve this with applesauce, balancing sweet and savory as well. In Switzerland, even a strenuous day spent hiking in the Alps is counterbalanced with a big pot of cheese fondue at the summit.

This perfect balance is what makes Swiss food such a joy to experience.

THANK YOU!

Apart from using recipe testers in both Switzerland and abroad, many recipes have been tested by you—the readers of my blog and cookbooks! In the past ten years, I've received so much insightful feedback: what works, what doesn't, and how your Swiss sweethearts and relatives do it in their kitchens. You've shared baking successes and failures, cooking wins and losses, legends and lore, and sometimes even a secret family recipe. I've connected with so many of you through Swiss food, and it has been absolutely delicious. Thank you.

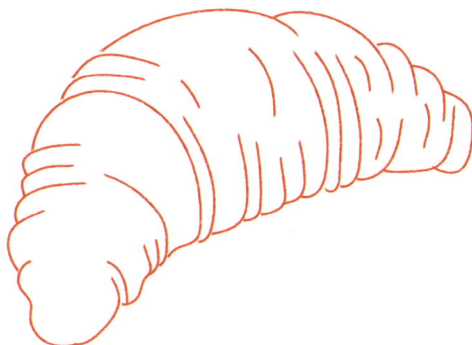

ABOUT THE AUTHOR

Love brought me to Switzerland—the love of fine baked goods.

I grew up in Calgary, Canada, but spent many childhood summers visiting my Swiss grandparents in Walenstadt, St Gallen. There, I experienced Swiss cuisine first-hand—biking to the local bakery for fresh *Gipfeli* (croissants), *Zopf* (braided bread) on Sunday, and *Wähe* (sweet and savory tarts) every Friday. After I trained as a pastry chef in Canada, the memories of the delicious food I'd sampled as a child made it clear that my best course of action was to return to Switzerland and learn how to make it all myself.

Love kept me in Switzerland, too.

I had intended to spend just a year in the country, but after moving to Bern in 2010 I met Sam, a bearded and bespectacled fellow cheese-enthusiast from the Entlebuch, and decided to stay.

In 2015, I started chronicling my Swiss food journey on my blog, *Helvetic Kitchen*. Since then I've been making, eating, writing about, enjoying, studying, sharing, and sometimes spectacularly wrecking Swiss dishes in an effort to encourage more people to try, and to appreciate, Swiss food.

I've posted hundreds of recipes over the years, many of which weren't easily available in English before. I've also written numerous cookbooks, including *Swiss Cookies* and *Alpine Elixirs* (which is all about Swiss drinks).

This cookbook is a collection of those culinary experiments. These recipes have mostly been gathered from my blog and cookbooks, and this new collection is meant to entice you further into the wonderful world of Swiss cuisine.

I've tried to prioritize ease—offering suggestions for how you can simplify a recipe while still retaining its authentic essence. If, however, you have further questions, or you want a step-by-step guide, most of the recipes have longer explanations and more background info on my blog, helvetickitchen.com.

Happy cooking! Happy baking! And happy eating too!

Andie Pilot
Trubschachen, Switzerland

SOME NOTES ON INGREDIENTS

Flour
Unless otherwise stated, recipes use regular white flour (*Weissmehl/ farine fleur/farina bianca*), similar to all-purpose flour.

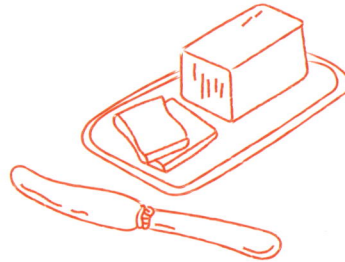

Butter
Recipes use unsalted butter with a fat content of 82%.

Sugar
Sugar refers to regular granulated sugar. Icing sugar refers to confectioner's or powdered sugar.

Dairy
Recipes use milk with a fat content of 2.5% and cream with a fat content of 35%. Either whipping cream or heavy cream can be used.

Eggs
I use "normal-sized" Swiss eggs, which typically weigh between 53–65 g (about 2 oz).

TIPS FOR SUCCESS

Weighing ingredients

Although I have included cup measurements here, I would recommend weighing ingredients with a scale for better accuracy.

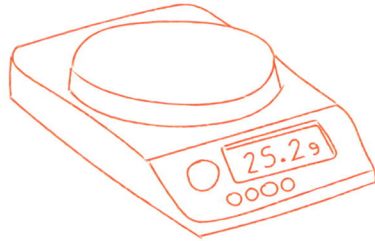

Oven temperature

The baking times and temperatures in this book were tested using a convection oven. If you have a conventional oven, you may have to raise the temperature by about 20°C/68°F, or bake slightly longer. Oven temperature and timing can vary wildly, so I have tried to give visual indicators (tops set, bottoms golden etc.), to help you know when to take things out.

Speaking of taking things out of the oven ... How do I know when my cake is ready?! One of the most difficult parts of baking is knowing when to take things out of the oven. The aroma of the cake is its siren song. Upon first scent, have a look through the oven window. Is the top set? If so, investigate further. Has it started to pull away from the sides of the pan? If so, press softly on the top. Does the cake spring back? It should fill the place where your finger was. If it does, your cake is probably ready. Let it cool fully in the pan.

Room temperature

Many recipes call for the ingredients to be at room temperature. For butter, this means you should be able to press into it and leave an indentation.

Here's a trick if the butter and eggs come directly from the fridge. Fill the sink with about 5 cm/2 in of very warm water and submerge the eggs. Break the butter into small pieces and put it in a medium bowl (or the one you'll use for mixing), then place it in the sink, making sure no water gets in the bowl. Stir and mash the butter occasionally until it softens, then it will be a good consistency for beating. Once the butter is soft, the eggs should also be ready to add to the recipe.

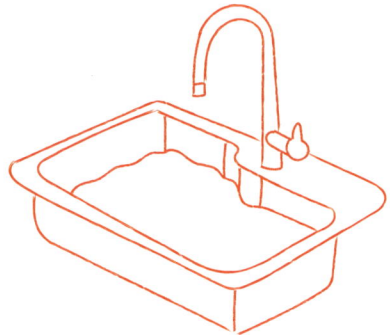

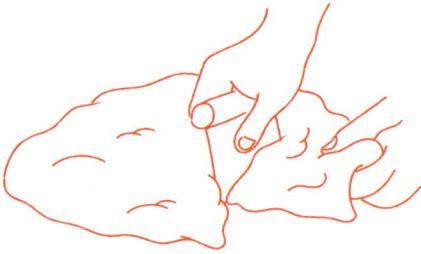

Cooling the dough

When it comes time to cool the dough, the best thing to do is split it into manageable pieces (about the size of your hand), wrap in plastic (or other reusable wrapper), and press down into a flat disc (this way it cools faster and is easier to roll out).

Cooling typically takes about one hour in the fridge or 15 minutes in the freezer. When it's time to roll it out, you might need to let it warm up for a few minutes on the counter, so that it's pliable again (this will depend on how cold the fridge is).

Whipping egg whites

Egg whites need time and attention in order to reach perfect fluffy peaks. Although the following isn't strictly necessary for all recipes that ask you to whip the whites, it's good practice for achieving light and airy end results, and essential when making baked goods like meringues.

Egg whites should be at room temperature, as this will help them reach full volume when whipped. If you need to use them right out of the fridge, let them sit in a small bowl of hot water for a few minutes before you crack them.

Be careful when separating the yolks from the whites, more than a small bit of yolk in the whites will inhibit their foaming ability.

Soft peaks are achieved when the mixture is glossy and forms droopy peaks—this is typically what you want when you are adding the whites to something like a cake batter or mousse. Stiff peaks are also glossy, but hold their form—this is what you want for meringues.

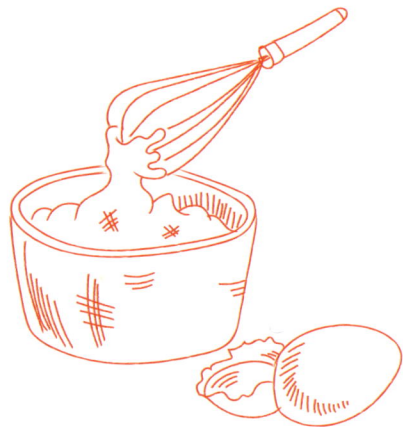

SOUPS AND SALADS

Soups are enjoyed in Switzerland year-round, but they are especially present in the fall and winter. You'll see them at autumn harvest festivals and frosty winter markets. There are carrot soups at Aargau's carrot market, onion soups at Bern's onion market, and chestnut soups from Ticino. Where I live, in the Emmental, we have a famous split pea soup for cold days that features cured pig's trotters, snout and tail.

The grape-growing regions spike their soup with wine, the cider-makers add apple juice and there are countless milk and cheese soups from the dairy farmers. There are soups to feed the poor, celebrate weddings, or strengthen new mothers who've just given birth. There's a soup for every occasion—and here you'll find a small selection to warm your chilliest days.

The Swiss love a salad. You'll find them in restaurants, served as an appetizer, main, or as a side to a *Fitnessteller* (basically the Swiss equivalent of a carb-free platter). Sometimes they skip the veg altogether, and make their salad out of sausages, cheese, or both! Here I've included a few varieties that you might like on the side, or as a whole meal.

WEINSUPPE — SOUPE AU VIN

An easy soup, starring wine!

Many of Switzerland's wine-producing regions make soups using white wine—you'll find them throughout the Valais, along Lake Biel, from Morges to Spiez. There's even a famous version from Solothurn, the *Soledurner Wysüppli*: an elegant soup with roots in the 16th century, when Solothurn was home to a succession of French ambassadors.

The aromatics in each recipe vary, but most versions involve a good amount of local wine and some cream to smooth everything out.

SERVINGS

2 as a main, 4 as a starter

INGREDIENTS

- 2 tbsp butter
- 1 carrot, finely diced
- 1 onion, finely diced
- 1 clove garlic, minced
- 1 thyme sprig
- 1 bay leaf
- 300 ml (1¼ cups) dry white wine
- 300 ml (1¼ cups) chicken stock
- 2 tbsp crème fraîche or sour cream
- 80 ml (⅓ cup) heavy cream

Garnish

- Chopped chives or edible flowers

METHOD

- In a large pot, heat the butter, then add the carrot, onion and garlic, and cook over medium heat until soft.
- Add the thyme and bay leaf. Deglaze with the wine, then add the stock and let simmer on low heat for about 10 minutes. Remove the thyme and bay leaf.
- Whisk together the crème fraîche and cream, then slowly whisk into the soup.
- Serve garnished with chopped chives or edible flowers.

TIPS

- Chasselas (known as Fendant in the canton of Valais) is a good wine choice for this soup.
- Pansies, nasturtiums, marigolds, and chive blossoms all make lovely edible flower garnishes.

BASLER MEHLSUPPE

Roasty, toasty flour soup

Fasnacht, or Carnival as it is known in many parts of the world, is the Christian celebration that comes right before the lean forty days of Lent. In Switzerland it's celebrated in the typical way: big street parties, loud music, parades, dressing-up, traditional fried delicacies, and plenty of drinking. Basel and Lucerne host the country's most famous events, with hundreds of thousands of people descending upon those cities for confetti-covered revelry.

A must during *Fasnacht* in Basel is their famous *Mehlsuppe* (flour soup). The most common origin story involves a chatty cook who burnt the flour during preparation. Instead of starting again, the mistake was added to the dish and became a great success.

SERVINGS

2 as a main, 4 as a starter

INGREDIENTS

- 3 tbsp butter
- 60 g (½ cup) flour
- 1 onion, minced
- 2 cloves garlic, minced
- 80 ml (⅓ cup) red wine
- 1 L (4 cups) vegetable, chicken or beef stock
- Salt and pepper
- Gruyère or other hard cheese, grated

METHOD

- In a large pot over medium, heat the butter. Whisk in the flour and keep whisking until the color turns chestnut brown. This can take up to 15 minutes.
- Once the flour mixture has browned, add the onion and garlic, cook for a minute, then slowly pour in the wine and whisk until smooth.
- Slowly pour in the stock and bring to a boil, whisking well—there should be no lumps.
- At this point, the soup is usually left on very low heat and cooked for another couple of hours to further develop its flavor. It can also be served right away.
- Season with salt and pepper and garnish with grated cheese.

TIPS

- If desired, you can puree the soup before serving.

SCHUPPA DA GIUTTA – BÜNDNER GERSTENSUPPE

Hearty Alpine soup with barley and bacon

There are 150 valleys in the canton of Graubünden and each probably has a different version of this, the region's most famous soup. The perfect warm-up after a long hike or day skiing in the mountains, it's easy to conjure up ... and filling to boot.

SERVINGS

4

INGREDIENTS

- 1 tbsp butter
- 3 medium carrots, diced
- ½ leek, sliced in rings
- 1 small celery root, diced
- 200 g (7 oz) bacon, cubed
- 60 g (2 oz) Bündnerfleisch, sliced
- 100 g (½ cup) pearl barley
- 1½ L (6 cups) beef stock
- Nutmeg, salt and pepper
- Splash of heavy cream (if desired)

METHOD

- In a large pot, heat the butter. Add the vegetables, meat, and pearl barley and fry over medium heat for about 5 minutes, or until the vegetables start to soften.
- Add the stock and bring to a boil, then lower the heat and simmer for about an hour.
- Season with nutmeg, salt and pepper. If desired, add a splash of cream to each bowl just before serving.

TIPS

- It's easy to make this vegetarian—just leave out the meat and use vegetable stock.
- If you don't have *Bündnerfleisch* or a similar dried meat, use more bacon.

SOUPE DE CHALET

Creamy Alpine soup with greens

Like the best Alpine dishes, *soupe de chalet* relies on ingredients that farmers would have had on the Alp, or calorie-rich items they could easily transport, like pasta. Most likely, they had access to a garden patch with onions and potatoes, and—of course—cream and cheese were abundant. Throw in a handful of wild spinach, nettles or wild herbs and you're cooking!

SERVINGS

4

INGREDIENTS

- 1 tbsp butter
- 1 onion, diced
- About 700 g (1½ lbs) potatoes, peeled and cubed
- 500 ml (2 cups) milk
- 1 L (4 cups) vegetable stock
- 150 g (5 oz) fresh or frozen spinach
- 2 tbsp herbs, finely chopped (like tarragon, mint, oregano, thyme, chives)
- Nutmeg, salt and pepper
- 150 g (1 cup) macaroni
- 75 ml (⅓ cup) heavy cream
- Gruyère or other hard cheese, grated

METHOD

- In a large pot, heat the butter. Add the onions and fry over medium heat until translucent, then add the potatoes and fry a minute more.
- Add the milk and stock, then the spinach. Bring to a boil, then lower the heat and simmer for about 30 minutes.
- Add the macaroni and herbs, and cook for about 10–15 minutes more, or until the pasta is tender.
- Stir in the cream, then it's ready to serve. Place some grated cheese in the bottom of each bowl and spoon the soup on top.

TIPS

- Most varieties of potatoes can be used; the consistency of the soup may just differ slightly. A floury/starchy potato, like those used for mashed potatoes, has a tendency to fall apart easier and may thicken the soup more. Waxy potatoes will hold their shape better.
- You can use other kinds of short, soup-friendly pasta, though the cooking time may vary slightly. Just check for doneness before adding the cream.
- I use a handful of grated cheese per bowl (about 30 g/1 oz), but you can use more or less depending on what you prefer—but don't leave it out! I think it makes the dish.

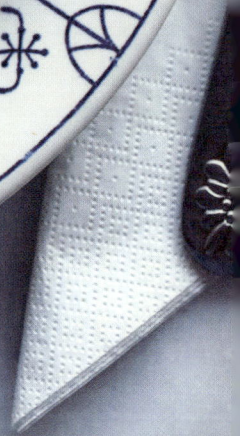

GEMISCHTER SALAT — SALADE MÊLÉE

A colorful collection of scrumptious salads

Served in restaurants as a starter, main or side, this is one of Switzerland's favorite salads. It's not one big mixed salad, but rather individual little salads arranged in colorful mounds on the plate—typically beets, carrots, celery root, corn, cucumber, and tomato (though numerous variations exist). The easiest way to make the salad is to make two base dressings and adjust them to the veggies as necessary.

SERVINGS

4 as a main, 6 as a starter

INGREDIENTS

Vinaigrette

- 150 ml (¾ cup) vegetable oil
- 80 ml (⅓ cup) apple cider or white wine vinegar
- 1 tbsp mustard
- 1 tsp honey (if desired)
- Salt and pepper

Yogurt dressing

- 120 g (½ cup) plain yogurt
- 80 ml (⅓ cup) vegetable oil
- 4 tbsp apple cider or white wine vinegar
- 2 tbsp mayonnaise
- 1 tsp mustard

METHOD

- Whisk everything together in a large measuring cup or bowl. Alternatively, you can measure everything into a jar, then close the lid and shake well. If the dressing appears thick, you can thin it out with a little water.
- This recipe makes enough dressing to dress all the salads below. Start by spooning about 3–4 tablespoons over each salad, and mixing well. Add more if needed. Leftover dressing will keep in the fridge for about a week.

Beet

- 2 large cooked beets, grated or cubed
- 1 medium apple, grated
- Vinaigrette

Carrot

- 6 medium carrots, finely julienned or grated
- Vinaigrette

Tomato

- 3 medium tomatoes, roughly chopped
- 1 tsp dried oregano
- Vinaigrette

Celery

- 1 small celery root, finely julienned or grated
- 2–3 rings of pineapple, chopped
- Yogurt dressing

Corn

- About 450 g (1 lb) tinned corn kernels
- 1 tsp yellow curry powder
- Yogurt dressing

Cucumber

- 1 cucumber, sliced in thin half moons
- ½ tsp dried dill
- Yogurt dressing

NÜSSLISALAT – SALADE DE MÂCHE

Hearty lamb's lettuce topped with bacon and eggs

The Swiss love *Nüsslisalat/Doucette/Formentino*. In English, these hearty bunched leaves are known as mâche, cornsalad, rapunzel or lamb's lettuce. Be sure to wash these little bunches of leaves thoroughly—they grow close to the ground and tend to accumulate grit and soil.

SERVINGS

2 as a main, 6 as a starter

INGREDIENTS

Dressing

- 150 ml (¾ cup) vegetable oil
- 80 ml (⅓ cup) apple cider or white wine vinegar
- 1 tbsp mustard
- 1 tsp honey (if desired)
- Salt and pepper

Salad

- 250 g (½ lb) *Nüsslisalat* leaves
- 4 hard-boiled eggs
- 12 bacon rashers, fried until crisp

METHOD

Dressing

- Whisk the dressing ingredients together in a large measuring cup or bowl. Alternatively, measure everything into a jar, then close the lid and shake well.

Salad

- Toss the leaves in a large bowl with the dressing. Slice the hard-boiled eggs and crumble the bacon, then add to the salad and toss lightly.

WURSTSALAT

Meat and cheese disguised as a salad

This "salad" hardly needs a recipe, but there is something so quintessentially Swiss about it, and not just because of the *cervelat*. The main ingredients—sausage and hard cheese—can be found in abundance in most Swiss refrigerators.

SERVINGS

4

INGREDIENTS

Salad

- 4 sausages (about 600 g/1¼ lbs), peeled and cut into half moons
- 200 g (7 oz) hard cheese, cubed
- 250 g (½ lb) cherry tomatoes, halved
- 8–10 radishes, chopped
- 2 tbsp fresh herbs, finely chopped (like chives, parsley, thyme)

Dressing

- 4 tbsp vegetable oil
- 2 tbsp white wine vinegar
- 1 tbsp yellow mustard
- 1 tbsp mayonnaise
- Salt and pepper

METHOD

Salad

- Mix the sausage, cheese, tomatoes, radishes, and herbs in a bowl.

Dressing

- Whisk everything together in a large measuring cup or bowl. Alternatively, you can measure everything into a jar, then close the lid and shake well.
- Pour over the salad, toss and serve.

TIPS

- In Switzerland the traditional sausage to use is *cervelat*, but if you can't find those then Lyoner sausage, or similar, will do.
- Infinitely adaptable, other great additions include rings of raw onion or sliced pickles.

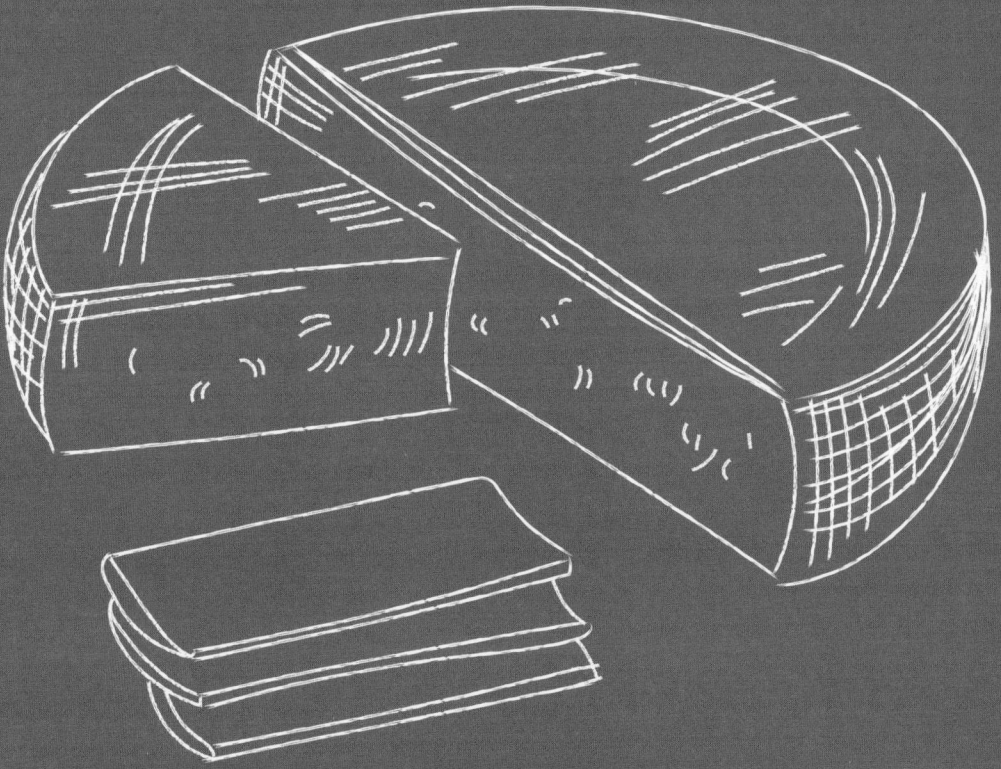

GLORIOUS CHEESE

In Switzerland, cheese is worth celebrating and the country's reputation as a cheese-lover's paradise is well-earned. They have been making cheese since Roman times and produce over 450 different varieties.

At any time of day, for any kind of occasion, the Swiss love an excuse to eat cheese. It can be sliced as thinly as paper and rolled into rosettes, like *Tête de Moine*. When the cheese is too hard to slice, like *Sbrinz* and *Berner Hobelkäse*, it will be planed off the wheel into rolls or chipped out as salty little nuggets. They'll eat the freshest cheese, *Ziger/Serac*, in big wet blocks, or cheese that's been kept in cellars and aged for nearly a decade. They'll eat cheese like *Schabziger* that's deliberately green and flavored with blue fenugreek, or cheese like Appenzeller, which is made according to a centuries-old secret recipe. If they need an excuse for a party, they'll melt the cheese and scrape it over potatoes, or make a big pot of the melted stuff and share it together.

If you need an excuse to eat cheese, then the next few pages are for you!

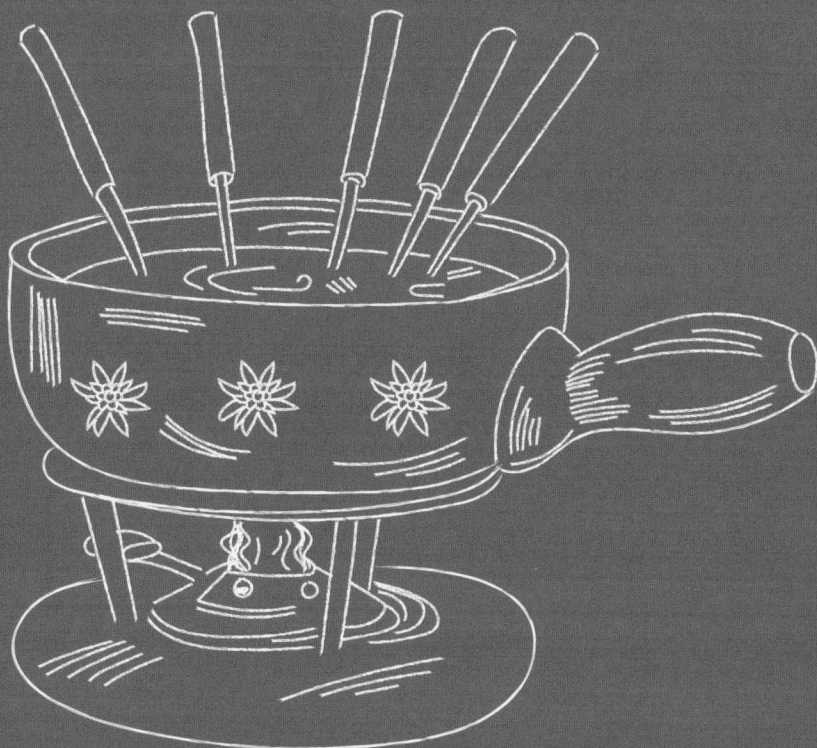

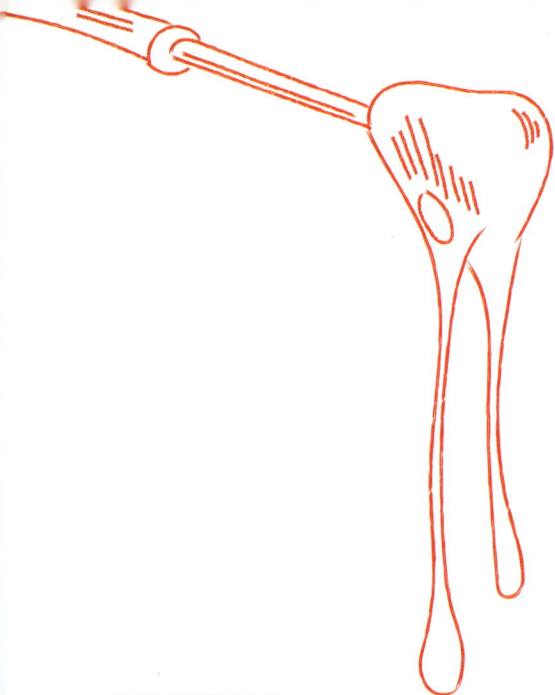

FONDUE

Whether as part of the holiday season, a work party, or after a day of hiking or skiing, the Swiss love a good cheese fondue. With convenient bagged cheese and specialty mixes from local dairies, as well as easy-to-portion bread and shops selling plenty of jars of pickles and onions, fondue in Switzerland is practically fast food.

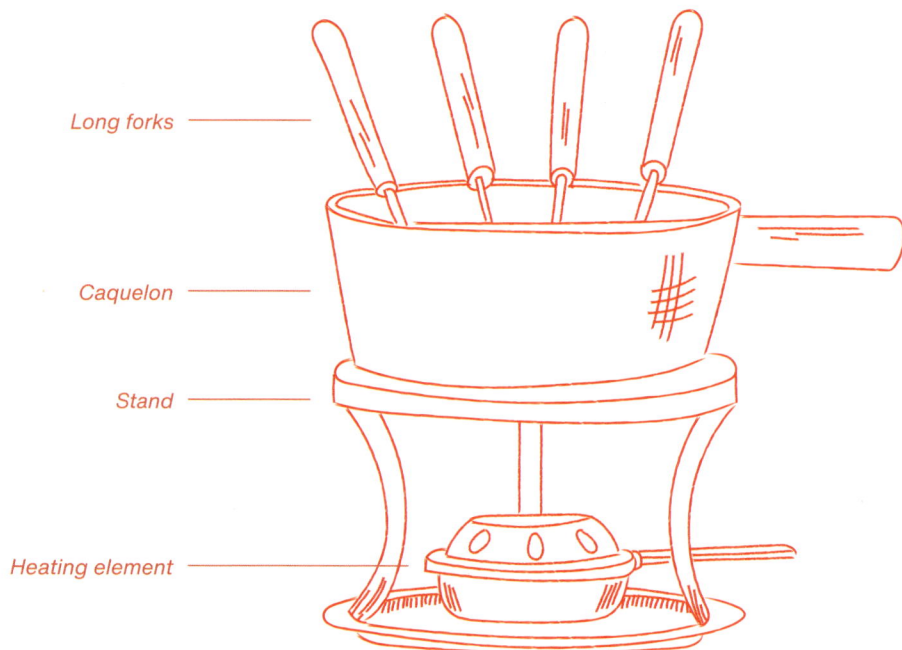

Chasselas

Long forks

Caquelon

Stand

Heating element

SO, YOU'RE HAVING A FONDUE ...

What equipment do I need?

You need a fondue pot, called a *caquelon*. Often made from ceramic or enamel, it allows the cheese to melt slowly. Then, you need a stand and a heating element. The heating element is a metal burner where you can add a flammable gel paste (or maybe you have an electric fondue set, those exist too!). Finally, you'll need long forks for dipping.

One fork, or two?

Most families dip and eat with one fork each, but if you don't know your fellow cheese eaters so well, or if you're feeling unwell, dip with one fork and use another for eating.

What drinks should I serve?

White wine is a perfect match for fondue. Typically, people drink Chasselas/Fendant, but a nice Amigne or Petite Arvine from the Valais would also suit. Alongside wine, warm tea is often served, purportedly to help digestion. Many people serve black tea, but in recent years I've seen more people serving herbal infusions, and you can buy fondue tea blends in many Swiss supermarkets.

Help! I've lost my bread!

It happens to the best of us! Every family seems to have a different approach to lost morsels. Some threaten dish duties for those who lose their bread, others a kiss. Among friends or colleagues you might be required to buy the next round of drinks.

The cheese is gone, now what?

When you get to the end of the fondue, you will probably find *s'Grosi* or *la religieuse*, the crispy cheese fixed to the bottom of the pot. For some it's the best part of the fondue, while others completely avoid this bleak reminder of how much cheese they've already eaten. If you're game, scrape it up and enjoy.

How do I clean this thing?

If no one's eaten the cheesy crust at the bottom of the *caquelon*, simply add enough cold water to cover the cheese, wait an hour, and then scrape it out using a paper towel or plastic scraper.

Ugh, now my whole place smells like cheese ...

Try leaving out a dish filled with ground coffee or plain white vinegar overnight.

But wait, how does fondue actually work?

The *caquelon* absorbs some of the direct heat and lets the cheese melt at the correct temperature. The more aged the cheese, the better it melts, and adding acid in the form of wine and lemon juice keeps the proteins apart and helps the cheese melt evenly. Finally, the cornstarch is essential to help bind the cheese and liquid together to produce the perfect consistency.

8

FONDUE

A great big pot of melted cheese

Nothing says Switzerland like cheese fondue.

SERVINGS

4

INGREDIENTS

- 2 garlic cloves
- 400 g (14 oz) Gruyère cheese, grated
- 400 g (14 oz) Vacherin Fribourgeois cheese, grated
- 300 ml (1¼ cups) white wine
- 1 tbsp lemon
- 1 tbsp kirsch
- 1 tbsp cornstarch
- Pepper and nutmeg
- Cubes of bread and/or small boiled potatoes for dipping

METHOD

- Set up the fondue stand and make sure you have enough fuel for the heating element.
- Cut the garlic into slices and use them to rub the inside of the *caquelon*. Leave the slices of garlic in the pot and add the grated cheese. Add the wine and lemon juice. In a small dish, whisk together the kirsch and cornstarch.
- Put the fondue pot directly on the stove and start to slowly melt the cheese over medium-low heat. Raise the heat a little and bring the mixture to a boil. Add the kirsch and cornstarch mixture, then bring back to a boil.
- Keep stirring until it all melts together and is bubbling.
- Season with pepper and nutmeg, then place the *caquelon* on the heated fondue stand, immediately beginning to stir with bread- or potato-skewered forks.

TIPS

- This version of fondue is known as *Moitié-Moitié* (half-half) because it is a mix of half Gruyère and half Vacherin Fribourgeois cheese.
- Use real (Swiss) cheese. If necessary, you can substitute with Emmentaler, Appenzeller or similar hard cheese. DO NOT use a generic "Swiss cheese"; these cheeses are mass produced and don't have the same melting properties (less smooth and creamy) and flavor profile.
- It will take a little while for everything to become a smooth, melted mass. However, if the fondue splits, whisk together about a tablespoon each of wine, lemon juice and cornstarch, and add to the pot, stirring over heat until it smooths out.
- Alcohol-free fondue? No problem! Replace the wine with dry non-alcoholic apple cider or alcohol-free wine, and leave out the kirsch entirely.

9

RACLETTE

Melted cheese scraped over potatoes

As the legend goes, herdsmen in the Alps used to lay their cheese wheels next to the fire and when the cheese got melty, scrape it onto their bread. It was the people from the canton of Valais, however, who coined the term *racler*, from the French word "to scrape," and devised the way it's eaten today.

Nowadays you can use an electric raclette oven, but in a pinch you can also melt the raclette under the broiler in the oven or even over an open fire.

INGREDIENTS PER PERSON

- About 200 g (7 oz) raclette cheese, in slices
- About 200 g (7 oz) small potatoes, boiled in their skins

Seasoning

Freshly ground pepper, paprika, curry powder, garlic powder, roasted onions

METHOD

- The most common way to eat raclette is using an electric oven to melt the slices. Many people add things on top of the cheese while it's grilling, like raw onions, pineapple, bacon, apples, or pears.

ON THE SIDE

- One of the best parts of raclette is the many sides served alongside the cheese. Some classic options include: pickles, cornichons, pickled onions (pearl and Borretane), pickled baby corn, stuffed peppers, pickled pumpkin or zucchini, or even dried meats like *Bündnerfleisch* and *Mostbröckli*.

TIPS

- A white wine like Fendant/Chasselas is usually served with raclette.
- Leftover raclette cheese can be used the next day for melted-cheese sandwiches or to top a casserole, and leftover potatoes are perfect for making Rösti (p. 51).

10

KÄSESCHNITTE – CROÛTE AU FROMAGE

Open-faced grilled cheese

There is nothing better than a cheesy, open-faced sandwich (until you put a fried egg on top).

SERVINGS
4

INGREDIENTS

- 200 g (2 cups) Gruyère or other hard cheese, grated
- 2 eggs
- 4 tbsp quark or sour cream
- 2 tbsp mustard
- Pinch of nutmeg
- 4 thick slices of bread
- 250 ml (1 cup) beer
- 200 g (7 oz) ham
- 2 tomatoes, sliced

Topping

- 1 tbsp butter
- 4 eggs
- Salt and pepper

METHOD

- Preheat oven to 200°C/400°F/gas mark 6.
- In a medium bowl, mix together the cheese, egg, quark or sour cream, mustard, and nutmeg. Set aside.
- Grease an oven proof dish (big enough to snugly fit the pieces of bread). Pour the beer into the bottom of the dish, then add the bread and turn once to soak. Place the ham on the bread, then a slice of tomato, then the cheese mixture on top.
- Bake for about 20 minutes or until the cheese mixture has melted and browned to your liking.

TOPPING

- In a small frying pan, heat the butter. Crack in the eggs, season, and cook on medium high heat until sunny side up. Season with salt and pepper and serve on top of the *Käseschnitte*.

TIPS

- Beer styles such as ale work well (including non-alcoholic versions). In place of beer you could also use white wine, dry cider or milk.
- You can use different kinds of ham, like leftovers from a roast or cold cuts. Of course bacon would also be delicious, or just leave out the meat for a veggie-friendly meal.

11

ÄLPLERMAGRONEN

Alpine macaroni with cheese and potatoes

The Swiss *Älpler* (herdsmen) traditionally spent their summers high in the Alps, as their cows grazed the meadows. Sitting around a fire with a big pot of fresh, boiling milk, they would make *Älplermagronen*—a creamy pasta with cheese and potatoes—which would have been wonderfully filling after a hard day's work.

Dried pasta was a good energy source, and lightweight, so it could easily be carried up to the Alp on a *Räf*, a wooden backpack. The pasta complemented the food that was available on the Alp, like potatoes, cheese and milk. Ladled into bowls, the *Älpler* might add sausages, onions or applesauce to their *Älplermagronen*, which was sure to keep them warm in the crisp mountain air.

Can't be bothered with potatoes? You'll find a recipe for *Chäshörnli*—straight macaroni and cheese—on the next page.

SERVINGS

4

INGREDIENTS

- 300 g (10 oz) potatoes
- Pinch of salt
- 300 g (3 cups) macaroni
- 750 ml (3 cups) milk
- 1 stock cube
- 200 g (2 cups) Gruyère or other hard cheese, grated
- Nutmeg, salt and pepper

METHOD

- Peel and cube the potatoes to about 1cm (½ in). Place the potatoes in a large pot and add enough water so they are just covered, then add the salt and bring to a boil. Let cook on high for about 5 minutes.
- Add the macaroni, milk and stock cube. Stir well.
- Cook for about 10 minutes. Keep an eye on the pot and if it looks a bit dry, add some additional milk or water and give it a stir.
- Once the pasta is cooked, add the cheese and mix well. If you like a saucier macaroni, add a splash of milk. Season with nutmeg, salt and pepper.

TIPS

- Most varieties of potatoes can be used, but the consistency of the dish may differ slightly. A floury/starchy potato, like those you use for mashed potatoes, has a tendency to fall apart easier. Waxy potatoes will hold their shape better.
- You can use either a chicken or vegetable stock cube: one that makes about 500 ml (2 cups) of stock.
- Serve with applesauce, fried onions, fried *cervelat*, or crispy bacon.

12

CHÄSHÖRNLI

Swiss mac and cheese

Beloved in Appenzell, and sometimes served with *Siedwurst*, a pale white sausage with a hint of caraway, *Chäshörnli* is a creamy, cheesy, straightforward macaroni and cheese. *Chäs* is the Swiss-German word for "cheese," and *Hörnli* means "little horns," describing the shape of the macaroni.

SERVINGS
4

INGREDIENTS

- 500 g (about 1 lb) macaroni
- 1 tbsp butter
- 1 tbsp flour
- 400 ml (1²/₃ cups) milk
- 200 g (2 cups) Appenzeller or other hard cheese, grated
- Nutmeg, salt and pepper

METHOD

- Bring a big pot of salted water to the boil, then add the pasta. Once it has cooked, strain the pasta into a colander and put the empty pot back on the stove over medium heat. Add the butter and as soon as it's sizzling, sprinkle over the flour. Whisk well.
- Once the flour has been incorporated, slowly pour in the milk, still whisking, then add the cheese. Stir until everything is creamy and uniform, then add the nutmeg, salt and pepper. Add the pasta back to the pot and give everything a good stir.

TIPS

- You can use other kinds of short pasta, like penne, rigatoni or fusilli. The cooking time may vary slightly, so check the packaging.
- Serve with applesauce and fried onions. Or garnish with chives.
- If the sauce is too thick for your liking, even it out with a splash more milk.

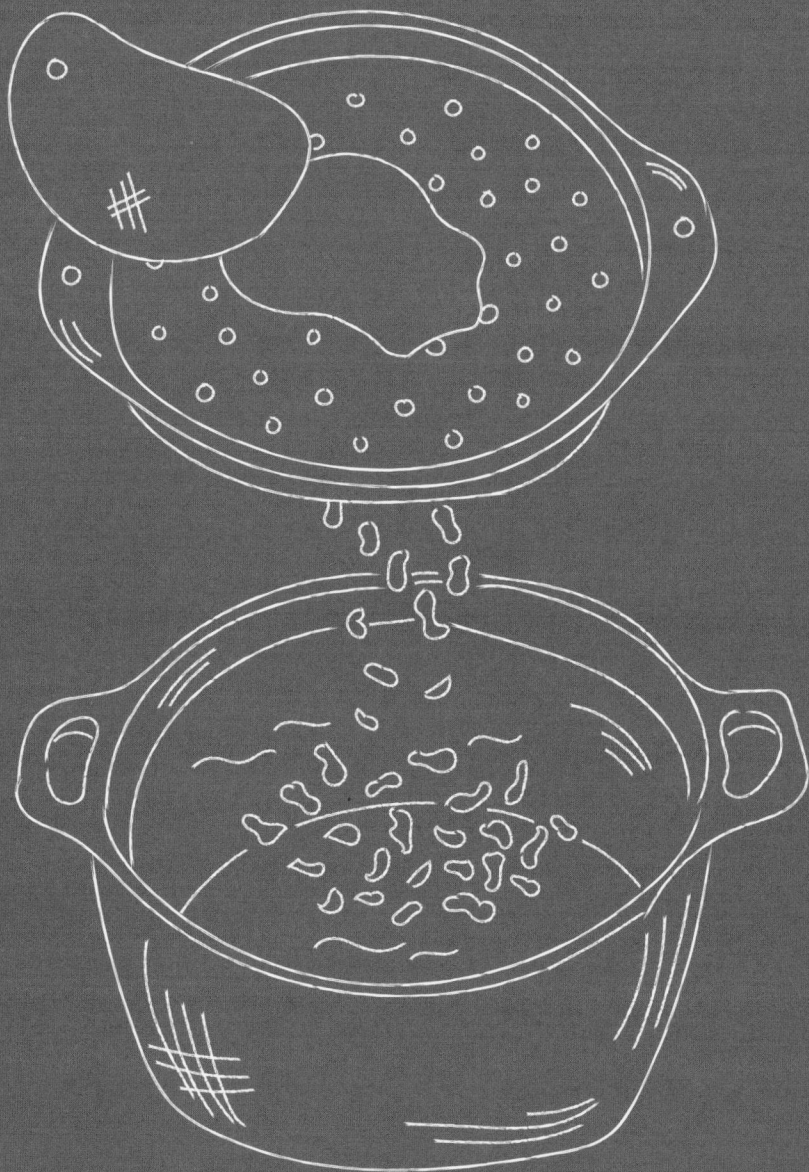

SIDES

These starchy sides are suited to accompany many different mains, from saucy stews to succulent sausages. However, they also have main-character potential. The simple additions of some fried eggs or fine cheeses make these dishes a more-than-acceptable main course.

Here you'll find four classic Swiss side dishes, including the world-famous potato fried pancake, Rösti (as well as a version from Graubünden that you can make in the oven). Creamy polenta from Ticino is a hearty favorite and pairs just as well with Alpine cheeses as it does with rich stews and sauces. And don't forget the perennial Swiss-German favorite: *Spätzli/Knöpfli*—little dumplings, boiled and then fried—that are the most perfect way to sop up everything from runny egg yolks to *Wildpfeffer* (marinated game meat).

13

RÖSTI

A golden and glorious fried potato pancake

Originally a farmer's breakfast, the Swiss now enjoy this grated, fried potato pancake at any time of day, either as its own meal or as a side dish. Its name is also used in reference to the imaginary barrier between the German- and French-speaking parts of Switzerland. *Röstigraben* (Rösti ditch) denotes the linguistic, cultural and political disparities that separate the two regions.

Don't have any cooked potatoes, or feel unsure about the flip? You'll find a recipe for *Plain in Pigna*—an easier potato pancake, baked in the oven—on the next page.

SERVINGS

2 as a main, 4 as a side

INGREDIENTS

- About 800 g (1¾ lbs) potatoes (see Tips)
- Nutmeg, salt and pepper
- 3 tbsp fat, like clarified butter or lard (see Tips)

METHOD

- Ideally a day (or two) before, boil the potatoes whole, in their skins. The potatoes should be cooked, but still a little firm. Cool them completely and store in the fridge until you're ready to use them.
- Coarsely grate the potatoes with a cheese grater or *Röstiraffel*, Switzerland's very own tool for grating Rösti potatoes. The skins should come off as you grate the potatoes (and can be discarded). Season with nutmeg, salt and pepper.
- In a large frying pan, heat 2 tbsp fat until sizzling. Add the grated potato, press it down into the pan and around the edges, and let it cook over medium for about 10–15 minutes.
- Use a spatula to peek underneath: if it's golden brown it's ready to flip over. Turn the whole pancake upside down onto a plate, add 1 tbsp fat to the empty pan, then slide the pancake back in. Cook for another 10–15 minutes.

TIPS

- Swiss supermarkets designate potatoes to use for Rösti, but a good choice outside of Switzerland would be Yukon Gold, Maris Piper or similar.
- The best fat to use is clarified butter. This allows you to cook at a higher temperature because the milk solids (that burn easily) have been removed. If you don't have this you can use lard, or just heat oil in the pan and add a little butter for flavoring.
- Leftover potatoes from a fondue or raclette make great Rösti.

14

PLAIN IN PIGNA

Rösti from the oven

Plain in Pigna is a traditional recipe from the Engadine valley in the canton of Graubünden. This dish removes the two most annoying aspects of Rösti-making—needing day-old boiled potatoes, and the dreaded flip. For this dish, you can use raw potatoes and bake it in the oven.

SERVINGS

2 as a main, 4 as a side

INGREDIENTS

- 800 g (1¾ lbs) potatoes
- 3 tbsp fine semolina or cornmeal
- 1 tbsp flour
- Nutmeg, salt and pepper
- 100 g (3½ oz) bacon, cubed
- 60 g (2 oz) Bündnerfleisch, diced
- 3 tbsp butter

METHOD

- Preheat oven to 200°C/400°F/gas mark 6.
- Peel and grate the potatoes. In a large bowl, mix together the grated potato, cornmeal, flour, nutmeg, salt, pepper, *Bündnerfleisch*, and bacon.
- Spread the mixture onto a parchment-lined baking sheet, then break the butter into little pieces and sprinkle over the top.
- Bake for about 30–45 minutes, or until it reaches your desired crispiness.

TIPS

- Use firm, waxy potatoes for this recipe—good choices outside of Switzerland would be Yukon Gold, Maris Piper or similar.
- If you don't have *Bündnerfleisch* or a similar dried meat, just use more bacon, or leave it out.

15

POLENTA

Creamy corn mash from Ticino

Polenta is yellow cornmeal that's cooked and stirred over low heat until it becomes a delicious, tender mash. It belongs, with chestnuts and risotto, to the traditional peasant foods of Ticino and can be eaten in many ways: right out of a bowl; spread on a wooden board to cool and set, and then cut with a piece of thin thread; or cooled completely in a form, then sliced and fried.

Served with butter, cheese, a stew, a sauce, or simply a splash of cold cream, polenta is an excellent and filling dish.

SERVINGS

2 as a main, 4 as a side

INGREDIENTS

- 500 ml (2 cups) water
- 500 ml (2 cups) milk
- ½ tsp salt
- 2 thyme sprigs
- 2 rosemary sprigs
- 200 g (1 cup) medium or coarse cornmeal/polenta
- 1 tbsp butter

METHOD

- In a large pot, bring the water, milk, salt, and herbs to a boil.
- Add the cornmeal slowly, while whisking, and bring the mixture back up to a boil. Continue whisking and let cook for a few minutes.
- Reduce the heat to low and let the polenta cook for a further 45 minutes, stirring often.
- Check that it's cooked through (it should be creamy and tender), then remove the herbs, stir in the butter, and serve.

TIPS

- I like to use a mix of milk and water, but you can also use just one or the other.
- You don't have to constantly stand by the stove, stirring, but you should stir often. Keep a little jug of milk or water at hand, and add a little bit every time it looks a little dry.

16

SPÄTZLI/KNÖPFLI

Plump little dumplings

These little dumplings are the perfect side to a saucy dish. The word *Spätzle* (*Spätzli* in Switzerland) literally means "little sparrows", while *Knöpfli* is the diminutive word for "buttons" in Swiss German.

The recipe below describes using a *Spätzlihobel*, a tool for making *Spätzli* that looks like a cheese grater with a box on top. It sits over a pot of boiling water and the batter drips through the holes as you move the box back and forth.

However, there are lots of creative ways to make *Spätzli* without a special gadget. There is a technique where you place the batter on a wet cutting board and flick pieces into the water (typically for professionals and grandmothers). Some people use a colander or cheese grater and push the batter through. But if you plan to make *Spätzli* even a few times, it's probably worthwhile getting a tool like a *Spätzlihobel*, which is inexpensive and pretty indestructible.

SERVINGS

2 as a main, 4 as a side

INGREDIENTS

- 300 g (2⅓ cups) flour
- Pinch of salt
- 1 tbsp coarse or fine semolina or cornmeal
- 3 eggs
- Water

METHOD

- Whisk together the flour, salt and cornmeal in a large bowl. Crack three eggs into a large measuring cup, then top up with water until you have 400 ml (1⅔ cups) liquid. Whisk this well.
- Pour the liquid slowly into the dry ingredients and beat with a wooden spoon, vigorously, until bubbles begin to form on the surface. Cover and let rest for at least a half hour.
- Once the batter has rested, bring a large pot of salted water to a boil. Have a sieve or slotted spoon and a large dish ready to fish out the *Spätzli* as they float to the top.
- When you have a steady boil, place the *Spätzlihobel* over the boiling water. Ladle a couple of spoonfuls of batter into the metal box (until it's about half full). Run the box back and forth, allowing the batter to drip through into the water.
- Once the box is empty, remove the *Spätzlihobel* from the pot (you can set it over the bowl). The *Spätzli* are cooked once they float to the top, so skim the water and place them in the prepared dish. Repeat until all the batter is used. You can serve the *Spätzli* at this point, shaken to remove excess water, then fried until brown and crispy.

MAINS

In Switzerland, the main meal of the day is typically eaten at midday. Where I live, in the Emmental, many people still go home for lunch every day and eat a big meal together with their families. This meal is usually warm and often features meat or plenty of cheese.

Meat is popular but pricey in Switzerland, owing to high quality standards, for which most consumers are willing to pay. According to the Swiss Office of Agriculture, about 55 kg/121 lbs of meat are consumed per person, per year—about 150 g/5.3 oz a day.

Pork is Switzerland's first-choice meat, followed closely by beef. Many of the dishes in this chapter feature meat— wonderfully rich sausages from Vaud, a meat pie from Chur, a beef dish from the monastery of Einsiedeln, and a hearty stew with dried fruit from central Switzerland.

Although the Swiss don't eat as much fish (on average about 9 kg/20 lbs per person, per year; the country is landlocked, after all), the communities near lakes and rivers often have wonderful dishes featuring domestic fish. This chapter features perch from Lake Geneva, a favorite of the region.

And don't forget the mountains! You'll also find recipes for two Alpine classics: *Capuns* from Graubünden and *Cholera* (no, not the bacterial disease, but a delicious savory pie) from Valais.

17

FILETS DE PERCHE

Fish doused in butter

A classic along the shores of Lake Geneva, these simple fish filets in butter are best enjoyed with a glass of cold, crisp, local Chasselas wine.

SERVINGS
4

INGREDIENTS

- 800 g (1¾ lbs) perch filets
- Salt and pepper
- 4 tbsp flour
- 125 g (½ cup) butter
- 60 ml (¼ cup) white wine
- Zest and juice of half a lemon
- Chopped parsley to garnish

METHOD

- Pat the fish filets dry and season with a little salt and pepper. Dredge them in flour, shaking off any excess.

- In a large frying pan, heat 2 tbsp of the butter. Add the fish in batches and cook over medium heat until golden (about 1–2 minutes per side). Keep warm in an oven on low heat (70°C/150°F).

- Once the fish has been cooked, add the remaining butter and lemon zest to the pan and let melt over medium heat. Then add the wine and lemon juice. Bring the heat up slightly and cook for 2–3 minutes, reducing the liquid.

- To serve, spoon the sauce over the fish and garnish with chopped parsley.

TIPS

- Serve with small, boiled potatoes or French fries.

18

PAPET VAUDOIS

Juicy sausages on a bed of leeks and potatoes

A classic in French-speaking Switzerland, *Papet Vaudois* consists of a base of leeks and potatoes topped with sausages, then simmered over low heat. The sausage juices drip down onto the potatoes and leeks, making them tender, meaty and flavorful.

Traditionally this dish is prepared with sausages from the canton of Vaud—either the pure pork variety, *Saucisson Vaudois*, or mixed with cabbage, as in the *Saucisse aux Choux Vaudois*. However, other smoked sausages with high fat contents, both Swiss and otherwise, also work.

SERVINGS

4

INGREDIENTS

- 1 tbsp butter
- 2 large leeks, cleaned and cut into rings
- 500 g (1 lb) potatoes, cubed
- 250 ml (1 cup) water
- 125 ml (½ cup) white wine
- Salt and pepper
- Boutefas, Saucisson Vaudois, Saucisse aux Choux Vaudoise, or other smoked sausages of your choice

METHOD

- In a deep and wide frying pan with a lid, heat the butter. Add the leeks and cook over medium heat for about 5 minutes, until softened. Add the potatoes, water and wine, then increase the heat and bring to a boil. Season with salt and pepper.
- Place the sausage(s) on top of the leeks and potatoes. Cover and simmer for about 25 minutes. Remove the lid and cook for an additional 5 minutes to let some of the liquid evaporate.

There are a few different ways to serve this dish:

- You can leave the whole sausage(s) on top of the leeks and potatoes and slice them at the table (bearing in mind that the sausages really squirt and should be poked with a sharp knife a few times to let some of the juices and fat run out).
- If you have more than one kind of sausage and want to sample them all, you may want to slice them in the kitchen and arrange them on top of the potatoes and leeks for serving.
- Some people squeeze out the sausage innards and mix them directly into the leeks and potatoes.

TIPS

- A Chasselas from the wine regions of Lavaux or Chablais is the perfect choice for cooking, and then drinking with the meal.
- The skin of the sausage is edible. Some people like to eat it, and some don't.

19

ZÜRCHER GESCHNETZELTES

Creamy veal stew

One of Switzerland's most famous dishes is this creamy stew, known as *Züri Gschnätzlets* in dialect. The word *Geschnetzeltes* simply refers to how the meat is cut—in strips. Technically, any kind of meat would be suitable (beef, chicken, turkey, pork), but veal is the favorite. It was probably used because, traditionally, it was an inexpensive meat; milk producers didn't have a use for so many young male cows.

Classic preparation involves the strips of meat being dusted with flour, fried, cooked in wine and stock, and simmered in cream. Mushrooms are usually in the mix (and sometimes kidneys), and an easy vegetarian alternative leaves out the meat completely. It is typically served with Rösti (p. 51).

SERVINGS

4

INGREDIENTS

- 1 tbsp butter
- 600 g (1¼ lbs) veal, cut into strips
- 2 tbsp flour
- 1 small onion, diced
- 250 g (½ lb) mushrooms, sliced
- 125 ml (½ cup) white wine
- 250 ml (1 cup) heavy cream
- 125 ml (½ cup) chicken or beef stock
- Zest of half a lemon
- Salt and pepper
- Parsley and chives, finely chopped

METHOD

- In a large frying pan, heat the butter. Dredge the veal in flour and fry in the butter for about 3–5 minutes over medium high heat. Remove from the pan.
- Add the onion and mushrooms to the pan and fry for a few minutes. Add the white wine, then the cream and stock. Lower the heat to medium and cook for about 10 minutes, or until you get a creamy, uniform sauce.
- Add the meat back to the sauce, stir in the lemon zest, then season with salt and pepper.
- Serve garnished with parsley and chives.

TIPS

- You can use different kinds of meat in this dish (generally anything quick-frying will do); or omit the meat, up the mushrooms, and use vegetable stock for a vegetarian alternative.

20

POT-AU-FEU – SPATZ

A one-pot meal from the Swiss army

The Swiss army has its share of iconic food items: from rations produced by some of Switzerland's premier cookie and chocolate factories (like Kambly and Frey, respectively), to *Militärkäseschnitte*, a bread battered with cheese and deep-fried.

However, no other dish represents the Swiss army better than *Pot-au-Feu/Spatz*—so much so, that it features on the cover of the current standard-issue Swiss military cookbook, ladled into a *Gamelle* (a standard-issue army food receptacle and cooking implement). It's a soupy stew of meat and potatoes, with plenty of vegetables to boot.

SERVINGS

6

INGREDIENTS

- 1.5 L (6 cups) beef stock
- 700 g (1½ lbs) boiling beef
- 1 onion
- 7 cloves
- 2 bay leaves
- 3 medium carrots, peeled and diced
- 1 large leek, cleaned and cut into rings
- 1 small celery root, peeled and diced
- ½ white cabbage, sliced
- 600 g (1¼ lbs) potatoes, cubed
- Salt and pepper

METHOD

- In a large pot, bring the beef stock to a boil and add the meat. Cut the onion in half and poke the cloves and bay leaves into it, then add to the stock. Let simmer over low heat for about 20 minutes.
- Add the vegetables to the pot, and simmer on low heat for about an hour.
- Add the potatoes and cook for an additional 30 minutes.
- Before serving, check to make sure the potatoes are cooked through, remove the onion with the cloves and bay leaves, and season with salt and pepper.

TIPS

- Good cuts of beef to use are brisket, shank or round.
- You are looking for a waxy potato here—something that won't break up while cooking. Good choices outside of Switzerland would be Yukon Gold, Maris Piper or similar.

21

EINSIEDLER EINTOPF

Creamy beef and leeks

This recipe comes from the Benedictine Abbey of Einsiedeln in canton Schwyz, one of Switzerland's most famous monasteries. A version of this dish has probably been eaten there since the Middle Ages.

SERVINGS

4

INGREDIENTS

- 500 g (1 lb) ground beef
- 1 tbsp butter
- 1 large leek
- 2 medium onions
- 300 ml (1¼ cups) beef stock
- 150 g (5 oz) herbed cream cheese
- Zest of half a lemon
- Salt and pepper

METHOD

- In a large frying pan over medium-high heat, brown the beef in batches, then remove from the pan and set aside.
- In the same pan, melt the butter, add the leeks and onions, and cook over medium heat until they soften slightly, about 5–7 minutes.
- Pour in the stock and let cook for a few minutes, then add back the beef. Let cook on low heat for about 15 minutes.
- Stir in the cream cheese and lemon zest, season with salt and pepper and then serve.

TIPS

- When browning the beef, to make sure it doesn't stick, you may want to add a little bit of oil or butter to the pan first, depending on how lean the meat is.
- You can use herbed cream cheeses like Boursin or Tartare.
- Serve with mashed potatoes, boiled potatoes or crusty bread.

22

SCHNITZ UND DRUNDER

Potato, pear and bacon stew

Schnitz und Drunder varies from region to region, but the contents are basically the same: potatoes, dried fruit, and bacon or smoked meat. Historically the use of preserved products meant that it could be made all winter long—which would have made sense for mountain dwellers who kept it simmering on open fires.

SERVINGS

4

INGREDIENTS

- 3 tbsp honey
- 250 g (½ lb) dried apples, pears or prunes, sliced
- 600 ml (2⅓ cups) chicken or vegetable stock
- 400 g (14 oz) smoked pork belly or bacon, cubed
- 700 g (1½ lbs) potatoes, cubed
- Salt and pepper

METHOD

- In a large pot, warm the honey over medium heat, then add the dried fruit.
- Pour in the stock, then add the meat. Simmer over low heat for about 30 minutes.
- Add the potatoes, making sure that they are submerged in the liquid (add a little more water if necessary). Simmer for an additional 30–40 minutes, or until the potatoes are tender. Season with salt and pepper.

TIPS

- Most varieties of potatoes can be used, but the consistency of the dish may differ slightly. A floury/starchy potato, like those you use for mashed potatoes, tends to fall apart easily. Waxy potatoes will hold their shape better.
- If the mixture seems a little dry after you've added the potatoes, just stir in a bit more water or stock.

23

CHOLERA

A savory pie stuffed with bacon, pears, cheese and more

There is a persistent rumor that this dish is, indeed, named for the cholera disease, after a particularly bad outbreak in the 1830s. People in the Valais stayed home to avoid contamination and were forced to use things they already had in their larder and gardens to feed their families.

Another possibility is that it's named after the glowing coal in the fireplace where the pan would have sat to bake (known in *Wallisertitsch*, the German-based regional dialect, as *Chola* or *Cholu*). Or perhaps for the *Cholära*, the part of the bakehouse where they stored the coals, and where the dish rested before baking.

SERVINGS

6

INGREDIENTS

- 300 g (10 oz) bacon, sliced
- 2 medium onions, diced
- 1 large leek, sliced into rings
- Nutmeg, salt and pepper
- 2 packages puff pastry, about 250–300 g (8–10 oz) each
- 3 medium apples, thinly sliced
- 3 medium pears, thinly sliced
- 400 g (14 oz) raclette or other hard cheese, grated
- 500 g (1 lb) small potatoes, boiled and sliced

Egg wash

- 1 egg

METHOD

- In a medium pan, fry the bacon until crispy then remove from the pan and set aside. Add the leeks and onions directly to the bacon fat and fry for about 7 minutes or until softened. Season with salt, pepper and nutmeg.
- Line the bottom of a 28 cm (11 in) springform pan with parchment paper, then line the bottom and sides with one package of pastry. Poke the bottom of the pastry all over lightly with a fork.
- Preheat oven to 200°C/400°F/gas mark 6.
- Once everything has cooled, fill the pie in layers: apple, potatoes, cheese, onions and leeks, pears, bacon. Keep layering until you run out of filling. You can lightly sprinkle nutmeg, salt and pepper onto some of the layers, according to your taste. Cover with the second pack of puff pastry and seal the edges well. If there's extra dough, you can cut out shapes and decorate the top of the pie.
- In a separate dish, whisk the egg then brush the top of the pie. Bake for about 30–40 minutes, or until the top is golden.

TIPS

- If an ingredient is missing, don't fret! Substitute it with more of something else or omit it (although I wouldn't leave out the cheese!).

24

CAPUNS

Dumplings, simmered in cream

Capuns are typical Alpine fare, originating from the canton of Graubünden. They are basically dumpling batter, wrapped in greens, and simmered in milk or cream.

Although the ingredients are simple, the process can be time-consuming. Nowadays you can find casserole variations, which don't wrap, but spread, the batter, saving you some time (see *Capuns Gratin* on the next page).

SERVINGS

4

INGREDIENTS

Batter

- 3 eggs
- 150 ml (²⁄₃ cup) milk
- Nutmeg, salt and pepper
- 300 g (2¹⁄₃ cups) flour
- 100 g (3½ oz) Salsiz or salami, cubed
- 100 g (3½ oz) Bündnerfleisch, sliced
- 100 g (1 cup) Gruyère or other hard cheese, grated
- A few leaves of thyme, oregano and mint, and a sprig of rosemary, chopped

Chard leaves

- About 30 small Schnittmangold leaves, or 6–7 large Swiss chard leaves each cut into 3–5 pieces

Continued next page

METHOD

Batter

- In a large bowl, whisk together the eggs, milk and seasonings. Add the flour while whisking, and then continue to whisk hard enough so you can see the batter bubbling up from the bottom. Stir in the meat, cheese and herbs. Cover and let sit for at least half an hour.

Chard leaves

- Bring a large pot of water to a boil. Add the leaves in batches, letting them soften for about 20–30 seconds, then fish them out and gently dip them in cold water. Carefully spread out the leaves and place them on a clean tea towel.

Assembly

- Place a softened chard leaf in your hand and put about a tablespoon of batter on top. Fold over the two edges lengthwise, then the top and bottom. Put these bundles directly into a large ovenproof frying pan.
- Preheat oven to 200°C/400°F/gas mark 6.
- Add the stock and milk to the frying pan with the *Capuns* and bring to a low simmer. Cook for about 15 minutes, or until the *Capuns* are firm. Pour the cream over the top, sprinkle with *Bündnerfleisch* and cheese, and put in the oven for about 15 minutes, or until the cheese has melted and the sauce is bubbling.

Continued next page

Cooking

- 250 ml (1 cup) chicken or vegetable stock
- 250 ml (1 cup) milk

Garnish

- 80 ml (⅓ cup) heavy cream
- Bündnerfleisch or Salsiz, sliced in strips
- Gruyère or other hard cheese, grated

TIPS

- Traditionally, *Capuns* are made with a leafy green known as *Schnittmangold*, a once-popular plant that fell out of favor, as spinach asserted dominance, but is now making a comeback. These leaves, about the size of your hand, are the perfect wrapping material for *Capuns* and are available in Switzerland from about May to September. If you're using these, simply snip off the stems and start rolling.

- For those who want to make *Capuns* outside of the season, or who don't have access to *Schnittmangold*, another option is to use *Krautstiel* leaves (Swiss chard; pictured) instead. Swiss chard is available from March to October, and adds an earthy flavor too.

- If you don't have *Bündnerfleisch*, *Salsiz* or a similar dried meat, you could use bacon, or leave meat out entirely for a vegetarian dish.

25

CAPUNS GRATIN

An easier version of the classic dish

Although there is no agreement on filling or method, it is clear that *Capuns* come from Surselva, a district in the west of canton Graubünden. Originally this was food for peasants, but now it is a specialty—served in restaurants throughout the region and loved by tourists and locals alike. You'll find the traditional method on the previous page, but this method, which spreads instead of wraps the batter, is an easy alternative.

SERVINGS

4

INGREDIENTS

Batter

- 3 eggs
- 250 ml (1 cup) milk
- 300 g (2⅓ cups) flour
- 100 g (1 cup) Gruyère or other hard cheese, grated
- 2 tbsp herbs, finely chopped (like mint, thyme, oregano, basil)

Assembly

- 6–7 large Swiss chard leaves, stems removed
- 250 ml (1 cup) milk or cream (or half and half)
- 100 g (1 cup) Gruyère or other hard cheese, grated

METHOD

Batter

- In a large bowl, whisk together the eggs, milk and seasonings. Add the flour while whisking, and then continue to whisk hard enough so you can see the batter bubbling up from the bottom. Stir in the cheese and herbs. Cover and let sit for at least half an hour.

Chard leaves

- Bring a large pot of water to a boil. Add the leaves in batches, letting them soften for about 20–30 seconds, then fish them out and gently dip them in cold water. Carefully spread out the leaves and place them on a clean tea towel.

Assembly

- Preheat oven to 190°C/375°F/gas mark 5.
- Grease a 2.5 liter (10 cup) casserole dish. Place a thin layer of batter at the bottom, spreading carefully, then place chard leaves on top. Keep alternating between batter and chard until it is all used up. Pour over the milk/cream mixture and top with the grated cheese.
- Bake for about 35 minutes or until the top is browned and bubbling.

TIPS

- This recipe is vegetarian, though you could add always add some diced *Salsiz*, *Bündnerfleisch*, or other cured meat or ham.

26

ZIBELEWÄHE – QUICHE AUX OIGNONS

A tart with a creamy, slightly sweet onion filling

Onion tarts are popular in different regions of Switzerland, but the most famous is probably the *Zibelechueche* from Bern, which features at the city's famous onion market in November. Another variation is the *Bölletünne* from Schaffhausen with bacon.

SERVINGS

4

INGREDIENTS

Dough

- 200 g (1⅔ cups) flour
- Pinch of salt
- 80 g (⅓ cup) butter, cold
- 125 ml (1/2 cup) water, cold

Filling

- 800 g (1¾ lbs) yellow onions
- 2 tbsp butter
- 125 ml (½ cup) milk
- 125 ml (½ cup) heavy cream
- 3 eggs
- Nutmeg, salt and pepper
- 2 tbsp breadcrumbs

METHOD

Dough

- In a large bowl, whisk together the flour and salt. Add the cold butter in pieces and rub into the flour mixture with your fingers until you have small flakes. Make a well in the middle of the flour, add the water and mix gently until a dough forms. Shape the dough into a disc, wrap, and let cool in the fridge for about an hour.
- Roll out the dough and line a 28 cm (11 in) round tart pan. Poke the bottom of the dough all over lightly with a fork, then keep cool until you have the filling ready.

Filling

- Cut the onions in half and slice them lengthwise. In a large frying pan, heat the butter, then add the onions and cook over medium-low heat for about 15 minutes, or until they are soft and transparent. Let cool.
- Preheat oven to 200°C/400°F/gas mark 6, bottom heat.
- Whisk together the milk, cream, eggs, and seasonings. Place the tart pan on a baking sheet. Sprinkle the bottom of the tart with breadcrumbs, spread the cooled onions in an even layer on top, then pour in the milk and egg mixture.
- Bake in the bottom part of the oven for about 40–45 minutes, or until the top has browned lightly and the filling is set.

TIPS

- To save time, you can use store-bought dough.
- Add 100 g (3.5 oz) diced bacon to the onions, and you'll have a version of the *Bölletünne*.

27

CHURER FLEISCHTORTE

The meatiest of meat pies

Chur, often advertised as Switzerland's oldest city, is the home of this meaty pie. With a filling of milk-soaked bread, bacon, ground meat, and a healthy splash of red wine, it's especially nice in winter and perfect on a chilly day after wandering the city's old town.

SERVINGS

6–8

INGREDIENTS

Dough

- 400 g (3⅓ cups) flour
- 2 tsp salt
- 150 g (⅔ cup) butter, cold
- 250 ml (1 cup) cold water

Filling

- 250 ml (1 cup) milk
- 250 g (3⅓ cups) leftover bread, cubed
- 100 g (3½ oz) bacon, diced
- 1 onion, diced
- 2 cloves garlic, minced
- 700–800 g (1½–1¾ lbs) ground pork, beef or a mix
- 1 tsp Dijon mustard
- 1 tsp each of dried thyme, marjoram and oregano
- 125 ml (½ cup) red wine or stock
- Salt and pepper

Egg wash

- 1 egg

METHOD

Dough

- In a large bowl, whisk together the flour and salt. Add the cold butter in pieces and rub into the flour mixture with your fingers until you have small flakes. Make a well in the middle of the flour, add the water and mix gently until a dough forms. Shape the dough into a disc, wrap, and let cool in the fridge for about an hour.

Filling

- In a medium pot, heat the milk until simmering. Remove from the heat and add the bread. Let sit until softened; about 10 minutes.
- In a large pan over medium heat, fry the bacon. Once it has browned a little, add the onion, fry until translucent, then add the garlic.
- Add the ground meat and brown for about 3 minutes (do this in batches if you have a small pan). Stir in the mustard and herbs.
- Pour in the wine, let simmer for about a minute, then take off the heat and season with salt and pepper. Add the milky bread and mix well. Let cool.
- Preheat oven to 200°C/400°F/gas mark 6.
- Roll out two thirds of the dough and line a 26 cm (10 in) round springform pan. Poke the bottom of the dough all over lightly with a fork.
- Roll out the remaining third of the dough into a 26 cm (10 in) disc. Fill the pan with the meat mixture, then place the disc on top and press down around the edges, sealing the pie. Brush the top with egg wash.
- Bake in the bottom part of the oven for about 40–45 minutes, or until the tart is nicely browned.

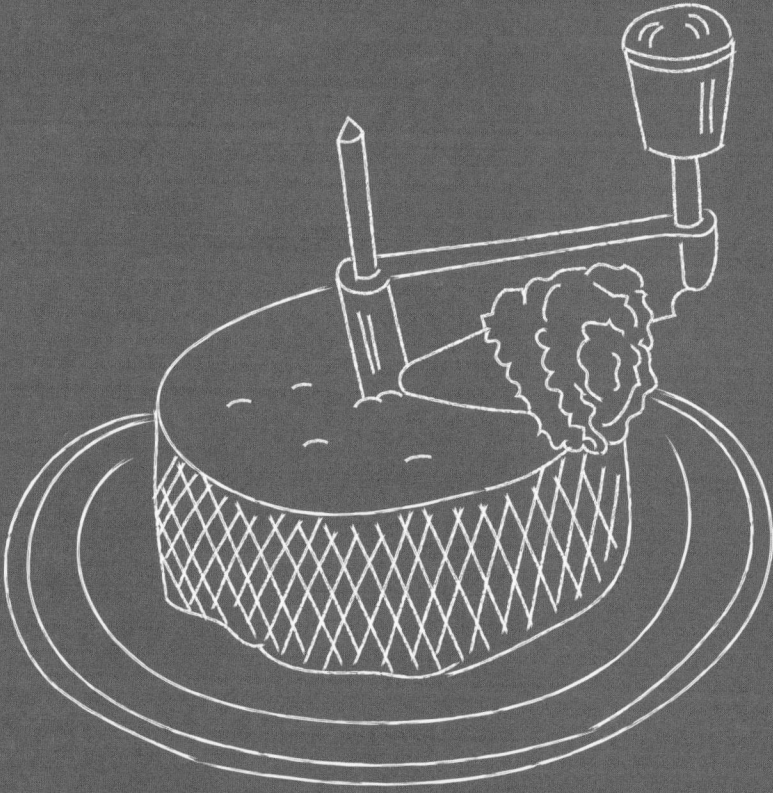

APÉRO

The next few recipes are perfect for an *Apéro*, and if you've lived in Switzerland for any amount of time, you've probably been to your fair share of them.

The Swiss like any excuse to hold one of these wine-fueled gatherings—weddings, birthdays, or simply *Feierabend* (the end of the working day). There is no event too small to accommodate an *Apéro*.

At the most basic *Apéro* there are glasses of cold white wine and little bowls of chips, peanuts or pretzels to nibble on. Sometimes an *Apéro* involves cheese, with cubes of *Sbrinz* and rosettes of *Tête de Moine*, accompanied by crackers or bread.

The most impressive and filling are *Apéro Riche*, where all manner of hors d'oeuvres and warm dishes are served, and it's perfect for when the party coincides with a mealtime.

No *Apéro*? No problem! These dishes can all be served as a main as well, and pair wonderfully with salad.

28

TOÉTCHÉ

Bread topped with tangy sour cream

Toétché, which is simply the Jurassien dialect word for "cake," has been baked for over a century and is perhaps the canton's best-known dish. It consists of a bready base topped with sour cream, and pairs wonderfully with a glass of crisp white wine.

MAKES

1

INGREDIENTS

Dough

- 400 g (3⅓ cups) flour
- 2 tsp salt
- 250 ml (1 cup) milk, room temperature
- 20 g (0.7 oz) fresh yeast or 2 tsp dry yeast
- 2 tbsp butter, room temperature

Assembly

- 1 egg
- 250 ml (1 cup) crème fraîche
- 2 tbsp heavy cream
- Saffron (optional)

METHOD

Dough

- In a large bowl, whisk together the flour and salt. In a measuring cup, mix together the milk and yeast.
- Make a well in the flour and add the liquid ingredients. Stir this together until a dough starts to form, then add the butter and knead on a flat surface until smooth and elastic. Alternatively, mix for about 10 minutes in a stand mixer with a dough hook.
- Cover and let rise for about an hour or until the dough has doubled in size.
- Line a 26 cm (10 in) springform pan with parchment paper and grease the sides. Roll out the dough into a circle and place in the pan, gently stretching it to the edge.
- Let rest for about 30 minutes.

Assembly

- Preheat oven to 200°C/400°F/gas mark 6.
- Whisk together the egg, then reserve about 2 tbsp for brushing the dough. Add the rest to the crème fraîche and cream, whisking well. If desired, add a few threads of saffron, broken up between your fingers.
- Pour the cream mixture into the center of the dough, spreading it to the edge. Bake for about 20–25 minutes, or until the top is nicely browned.

29

SCHINKENGIPFELI – CROISSANTS AU JAMBON

Crisp, flaky croissants bursting with ham

Flaky on the outside and savory on the inside, these ham croissants are great for an *Apéro* or make a delicious quick dinner, paired with a salad.

MAKES
8

INGREDIENTS

- 120 g (½ cup) quark or sour cream
- 100 g (3½ oz) ham, diced
- ½ an onion, minced (about 2 tbsp)
- 1 clove garlic, minced
- 1 tbsp lemon juice
- Zest of 1 lemon
- 1 tsp mustard
- Thyme, salt and pepper
- 320 g (11 oz) puff pastry
- 1 egg, separated

METHOD

- Preheat oven to 200°C/400°F/gas mark 6.
- Mix together the quark or sour cream, ham, onion, garlic, lemon juice and zest, mustard, and seasonings.
- Roll out the puff pastry into a circle about 32 cm (12½ in), slice into eight wedges and brush with egg white.
-
  Add a heaping tablespoon of filling to the middle of each wedge, then roll up the dough into the shape of a croissant. Place on a parchment-lined baking sheet, then brush with egg yolk.
- Bake for about 20–25 minutes, or until the pastry has puffed and the outside is golden.

TIPS

- Want a vegetarian alternative? Swap the ham for cheese.

CHÄSCHÜECHLI – RAMEQUINS AU FROMAGE

You won't find cheesier tarts

Difficult to pronounce, but easy to eat, these little cheese tarts are an absolute Swiss classic, and one that you'll find in all corners of the country.

The real secret is the cheese, and it's worth experimenting to find your favorite (though both Appenzeller and Gruyère are good choices in a pinch, or you can use a mix of different hard cheeses). Another game-changer is the pastry. While store-bought is perfectly fine, a buttery, homemade version makes for the stuff of cheese-tart dreams.

MAKES

12

INGREDIENTS

Dough

- 160 g (1¼ cups) flour
- 1 tsp salt
- 60 g (¼ cup) butter, cold
- 100 ml (⅓ cup + 1 tbsp) water

Filling

- 2 eggs
- 125 ml (½ cup) milk
- 125 ml (½ cup) heavy cream
- Nutmeg, salt and pepper
- 120 g (1¼ cups) Gruyère or other hard cheese, grated

METHOD

Dough

- In a large bowl, whisk together the flour and salt. Add the cold butter in pieces and rub into the flour mixture with your fingers until you have small flakes.
- Make a well in the middle of the flour, add the water and mix gently until a dough forms.
- Shape the dough into a disc, wrap, and let cool in the fridge for about an hour.
- Roll out the dough, cut large rounds of 11 cm (4 in), and line a standard 12-cup muffin tin. Poke the bottom of the dough all over lightly with a fork, then keep cool until you have the filling ready.

Filling

- Preheat oven to 200°C/400°F/gas mark 6, bottom heat.
- Whisk together the eggs, milk, cream, nutmeg, salt, and pepper.
- Place the muffin tin on a baking sheet, then add an equal amount of cheese to each cup. Pour the egg mixture into each cup about three quarters full.
- Bake for about 20–25 minutes in the bottom half of the oven, or until the tops are browned and the filling is set.

BOUNTIFUL BREAD

Little neighborhood bakeries still grace the main streets in Switzerland, from the bustling cities to the tiniest Alpine villages. The bread they sell is one of Switzerland's most important daily staples and, according to the Swiss Bread Association, 98% of the population consumes it; many on a daily basis.

There are over 200 different kinds of bread produced in Switzerland. There are breads for the daily feeding of families: from the standard, toothsome white and whole wheat breads to ones made with grains like spelt and rye. There are little milk buns perfect for skewering with sticks of chocolate, and pretzel buns that make the world's best sandwiches. There is special bread for feasting and celebrating, bread made to look like boys, bread spiced with saffron, bread hiding kings, and the king of Swiss breads—the beautiful, plaited *Zopf* that graces so many Sunday breakfast tables. You'll find all these breads on the following pages.

31

SOLOTHURNERBROT

Buttery braided bread

There is nothing more satisfying than the thick, crispy crust of Solothurn's cantonal bread, *Solothurnerbrot*. According to Elisabeth Pfluger, valiant chronicler of all things Solothurn, good Solothurners know not to press too much air out of the bread with overzealous kneading. They also know that to get that magnificent crust you don't cut the dough before it goes in the oven—just a simple fold to hold in all its airy goodness and to crisp up its outer shell.

MAKES

1

INGREDIENTS

- 500 g (4 cups) flour
- 2 tsp salt
- 330 ml (1⅓ cups) warm water
- 20 g (0.7 oz) fresh yeast or 2 tsp dry yeast

METHOD

- In a large bowl, whisk together the flour and salt. In another bowl, whisk together the water and yeast.
- Make a well in the flour, pour in the liquid, and using an electric or stand mixer with a dough hook, mix for about 10 minutes. It will be quite sticky. Cover and let rise for about an hour or until the dough has doubled in size. During this process, very gently fold the dough in half a couple of times to improve the structure. Since the dough is sticky, dip your hands in water before handling it.
- Once it has risen, dust the top of the dough with a little flour and gently form it into a ball while still in the bowl (trying not to squeeze out any of the air). Place it directly on a parchment-lined baking sheet, then make a light indentation in the middle of the dough and very lightly fold it in half.
- Let rise for 20–30 minutes.
- Preheat oven to 230°C/450°F/gas mark 8.
- Bake for about 45–50 minutes, or until the bread is nicely browned and it makes a hollow sound when tapped on the bottom.

TIPS

- For a super crispy crust, place a baking sheet on the bottom rack of the oven and as soon as you put the bread in, pour about 125 ml (½ cup) water into the baking sheet. The water evaporates and helps make the crust crunchy.

32

ZOPF – TRESSE

Buttery braided bread

Switzerland's most beloved bread is a plaited golden loaf called *Zopf/Tresse/Treccia* ("braid" in German/French/Italian). Many cultures have their own version of enriched braided bread, but the buttery version enjoyed in Switzerland today has its origins in Bern.

Bernese bakers began making *Zopf* (*Züpfe* in the Bernese dialect) in the late Middle Ages. By law, they could only produce it for the feast day of St. Thomas and for New Year's Day, but in 1629 the bakers petitioned the government and were granted the right to make it year-round.

MAKES

1

INGREDIENTS

Dough

- 500 g (4 cups) flour
- 2 tsp salt
- 250 ml (1 cup) milk, room temperature
- 20 g (0.7 oz) fresh yeast or 2 tsp dry yeast
- 1 tsp sugar
- 100 g (½ cup) butter, room temperature

Egg wash

- 1 egg
- Pinch of salt

METHOD

- In a large bowl, whisk together the flour and salt. In another bowl, whisk together the milk, yeast and sugar.
- Make a well in the flour and add the liquid ingredients. Stir this together until a dough starts to form, then add the butter and knead on a flat surface for about 15 minutes, or until it is smooth and elastic. Alternatively, mix for about 10 minutes in a stand mixer with a dough hook.
- Cover and let rise for about an hour or until the dough has doubled in size.
- Split the dough into two and roll each into a long strand. Cross the two strands in the middle, then braid a two-strand loaf (see Tips). Place on a parchment-lined baking sheet and let rise for about 30 minutes.
- Preheat oven to 230°C/450°F/gas mark 8.
- Whisk together the egg and salt, then brush the dough.
- Bake for about 30–35 minutes, or until the bread is beautifully golden and it makes a hollow sound when tapped on the bottom.

TIPS

- Two-strand is the most traditional way to braid *Zopf*, though numerous variations exist. If you need help, there are lots of how-to videos online.

33

GRITTIBÄNZ

Bready boys for St. Nicholas

Switzerland, like many parts of Europe, celebrates St. Nicholas Day on December 6, and *Grittibänz* are the featured baked good to go along with the day. Although they originated in the German-speaking part of the country, today they are widespread throughout, and known as *Bonhomme de pâte* in French and *Ometti di pasta* in Italian.

Gritti comes from the German word *grätschen* which translates as "splayed" or "straddled," describing the form of the legs, and *Bänz* is a short form of the extremely common 1800s name Benedict, which was used as a stand-in to describe any man (like the English name Jack).

Today you see a lot of bready boys, but historically there were plenty of bread girls, too. Have fun forming the figures however you like!

MAKES

5

INGREDIENTS

Dough

- 500 g (4 cups) flour
- 2 tsp salt
- 250 ml (1 cup) milk, room temperature
- 20 g (0.7 oz) fresh yeast or 2 tsp dry yeast
- 1 tbsp sugar
- 100 g (½ cup) butter, room temperature

Egg wash

- 1 egg
- Pinch of salt

Decoration

- Raisins and pearl sugar

METHOD

- In a large bowl, whisk together the flour and salt. In another bowl, whisk together the milk, yeast, and sugar.
- Make a well in the flour and add the liquid ingredients. Stir this together until a dough starts to form, then add the butter and knead on a flat surface for about 15 minutes, or until it is smooth and elastic. Alternatively, mix for about 10 minutes in a stand mixer with a dough hook.
- Cover and let rise for about an hour or until the dough has doubled in size.
- Preheat oven to 190°C/375°F/gas mark 5.
- Split the dough into six pieces, about 150 g (5 oz) each. Five will be for the *Bänz*, and the sixth can be used for decorations. Roll the dough into logs, then cut out the arms and legs, forming it into the shape of a person.

Continued next page

- Use the remaining dough to fashion buttons, hats, scarves, boots—whatever you fancy. Place these on the. If you are using raisins for eyes or buttons, be sure to place them deep into the dough so they don't fall off or burn during baking.

- Place the *Bänz* on a parchment-lined baking sheet and let them rise for about 20 minutes.

- Whisk together the egg and salt, then brush the dough. It's best to add pearl sugar now, so that it will stick to the egg wash.

- Bake for about 20–30 minutes or until they are golden and sound hollow when you tap their bottoms.

34

DREIKÖNIGSKUCHEN
GÂTEAU DES ROIS

Soft, spiced bread, studded with raisins

On Epiphany, January 6, it's traditional to eat a *Dreikönigskuchen*, known as *Couronne des rois* in French and *corona dei re magi* in Italian. This holiday celebrates the three kings finally reaching Bethlehem, so a small plastic king figurine (or whole almond) is baked into the bread. Whoever finds it is king for the day!

The tradition of hiding a token in baked goods is a long one, and similar customs exist all over Europe. The Swiss version has a clear origin—bread researcher Max Währen pitched it to the association of Swiss bakers in 1952. A modest success at first, the *Neue Zürcher Zeitung* reported that Migros supermarket alone sold 700,000 in 2023.

MAKES

1

INGREDIENTS

Dough

- 500 g (4 cups) flour
- 1 tsp salt
- 300 ml (1¼ cups) milk, room temperature
- 20 g (0.7 oz) fresh yeast or 2 tsp dry yeast
- 3 tbsp sugar
- 60 g (¼ cup) butter, room temperature
- Zest of 1 lemon
- Zest of 1 orange
- 100 g (¾ cup) raisins
- 1 whole almond

Egg wash

- 1 egg

Topping

- Slivered or sliced almonds and pearl sugar

METHOD

- In a large bowl, whisk together the flour and salt. In another bowl, whisk together the milk, yeast and sugar.

- Make a well in the flour and add the liquid ingredients. Stir this together until a dough starts to form, then add the butter, zest and raisins, and knead on a flat surface for about 15 minutes, or until it is smooth and elastic. Alternatively, mix for about 10 minutes in a stand mixer with a dough hook.

- Cover and let rise for about an hour or until the dough has doubled in size.

- Split off eight portions of dough, each about 80 g (2.8 oz), and roll each into a ball. Make sure to press an almond (or a plastic king figurine, if you have one) into the bottom of one of the balls, then pinch the dough together around it to seal it inside.

- Use the rest of the dough to form a bigger ball, and place this on a parchment-lined baking sheet. Place the eight smaller balls in a circle around it and let rise for 30 minutes.

- Preheat oven to 180°C/350°F/gas mark 4.

Continued next page

- Whisk the egg and brush evenly over the bread. Sprinkle with slivered or sliced almonds and pearl sugar.
- Bake for about 30–35 minutes, or until it is golden and makes a hollow sound when tapped on the bottom.

TIPS

- Supermarket and bakery *Dreikönigskuchen* generally come with a paper crown. For an authentic experience, make your own and force the king to wear it for the whole day.
- It's always nice to plump the raisins before adding them to the dough. You can do this in strongly brewed tea, or for something more adult, use rum or cognac. Let them sit while you prepare the other ingredients, then strain and use as indicated in the recipe.

35

WEGGLI – PETITS PAINS AU LAIT

Little milk buns

These little golden milk buns make a perfect breakfast, snack or sandwich, and leftovers. They are especially loved by children, and often paired with a hefty *Branche* (a stick of praline milk chocolate). Weggli are also traditionally eaten on August 1, Switzerland's national holiday, with a cross cut into the dough and a little Swiss toothpick flag on top.

In German-speaking Switzerland, when you want to say you can't have things both ways, you say, "You can't have both the *Weggli* and the *Füfi*" (the coin you need to buy it)— *Chasch ned s'Füfi und s'Weggli ha.*

MAKES

10

INGREDIENTS

Dough

- 500 g (4 cups) flour
- 2 tsp salt
- 300 ml (1¼ cups) milk, room temperature
- 20 g (0.7 oz) fresh yeast or 2 tsp dry yeast
- 1 tbsp sugar
- 60 g (¼ cup) butter, room temperature

Egg wash

- 1 egg
- Pinch of salt

METHOD

- In a large bowl, whisk together the flour and salt. In another bowl, whisk together the milk, yeast and sugar.
- Make a well in the flour and add the liquid ingredients. Stir this together until a dough starts to form, then add the butter and knead on a flat surface for about 10 minutes, or until smooth and elastic. Alternatively, mix for about 8 minutes in a stand mixer with a dough hook.
- Cover and let rise for about an hour or until the dough has doubled in size.
- Preheat oven to 200°C/400°F/gas mark 6.
- Split the dough into 10 pieces, each 90 g (3 oz) and roll into buns. Use the handle of a wooden spoon to make an indent in the middle of the bun— the indent should be very deep, but the dough should still be attached. Place on a parchment-lined baking sheet and let rise for about 20 minutes.
- Whisk together the egg and salt, then brush the dough.
- Bake for about 20 minutes, or until they are golden.

TIPS

- One of the best variations of *Weggli* is *Schoggibrötli/Petits pains au chocolat*: buns stuffed with chocolate. Simply add 150 g (5.3 oz) chopped chocolate to the dough after the butter is incorporated. Each piece will weigh about 115 g (4 oz) and you can replace the salt with sugar in the egg wash.

36

SILSERLI — PETITS PAINS DE SILS

Nothing beats a pretzel bun

A common complaint from homesick Swiss abroad is the lack of good bread. It was a recurrent refrain in our house in Calgary in the 80s and 90s, as my Swiss mother pined for robust crusts and tasty innards. But what did she miss most of all? Pretzel buns.

Often sold in rings of six, these little buns are perfect to bring along on picnics, serve alongside a soup or salad, or just butter generously and devour as an "anytime" snack.

It may seem intimidating to make them—before baking, you need to boil the buns in a baking soda solution—but the process is quite straightforward. If you have the time, they are definitely worth making from scratch and their flavorful crust and tender crumb will have any Swiss abroad longing for home.

MAKES
12

INGREDIENTS

Dough

- 500 g (4 cups) flour
- 2 tsp salt
- 300 ml (1¼ cups) milk, room temperature
- 20 g (0.7 oz) fresh yeast or 2 tsp dry yeast
- 60 g (¼ cup) butter, room temperature

Dipping solution

- 100 g baking soda
- 1 L water

METHOD

- In a large bowl, whisk together the flour and salt. In another bowl, whisk together the milk and yeast.
- Make a well in the flour and add the liquid ingredients. Stir this together until a dough starts to form, then add the butter and knead on a flat surface for about 10 minutes, or until smooth and elastic. Alternatively, mix for about 8 minutes in a stand mixer with a dough hook.
- Cover and let rise for about an hour or until the dough has doubled in size.
- Preheat oven to 200°C/400°F/gas mark 6.
- Split the dough into 12 pieces, about 70–75 g (2½ oz) each, then roll into buns.
- Meanwhile, boil the water in a large pot and add the baking soda.
- One by one, gently drop each bun into the boiling water and count slowly to 10. Use a slotted spoon or sieve to remove the buns, shake off excess water and place them on a parchment-lined baking sheet.
- Once they have all been dipped, make two cuts across the top then bake for about 20 minutes, or until they are a deep brown on the top and bottom.

FASTENWÄHE

Luscious little breads with a sprinkling of caraway

These little breads, typically sprinkled with caraway seeds, have long been associated with *Fastenzeit* (Lent) in Basel. They're served from *Dreikönigstag* on January 6 to Easter Sunday.

Popular in the region for over four centuries, today *Fastenwähe* are produced not only in Basel but all over Switzerland. You can even buy a special tool called a *Faschtewaije Yse* to cut out their signature holes (though a paring knife works just as well).

MAKES

12

INGREDIENTS

Dough

- 450 g (3⅔ cups) flour
- 2 tsp salt
- 300 ml (1¼ cups) milk, room temperature
- 20 g (0.7 oz) fresh yeast or 2 tsp dry yeast
- 125 g (½ cup) butter, room temperature

Egg wash and topping

- 1 egg yolk
- Caraway seeds

METHOD

- In a large bowl, whisk together the flour and salt. In another bowl, whisk together the milk and yeast.
- Make a well in the flour and add the liquid ingredients. Stir this together until a dough starts to form, then add the butter a little at a time. It will make the dough slick and greasy, but should eventually mix in. Knead this for about 15 minutes, or until you have a soft, smooth dough. Alternatively, mix for about 10 minutes in a stand mixer with a dough hook.
- Cover and let rise for about an hour.
- Preheat oven to 200°C/400°F/gas mark 6.
- Turn out the dough onto the counter and gently press out the air. Separate into 12 balls, about 80 g (3 oz) each, and let rest about 10 minutes.
- Press the balls down to make discs, then use a very sharp knife to cut four holes into each disc. Use your fingers to widen the holes and stretch out the discs.
- Place on a parchment-lined baking sheet and brush with the egg yolk. Sprinkle with caraway seeds, then bake for about 25–30 minutes or until golden.

38

CUCHAULE

Fribourg's famous saffron bread

During the fall, *Bénichon* is celebrated in the canton of Fribourg. Once a religious festival, it has broadened into an autumn folk festival which also celebrates the harvest and the return of the cows from mountain pastures. And like the best harvest festivals, it features plenty of good things to eat! *Cuchaule*, their famous saffron bread, is served with *Moutarde de Bénichon*, a spread made with pear syrup, white wine and spices. Once only available in the fall, nowadays you can find it year round in local bakeries.

MAKES

1

INGREDIENTS

Dough

- 600 g (4¾ cups) flour
- 80 g (⅓ cup) sugar
- 1 tsp salt
- 300 ml (1¼ cups) milk, room temperature
- 20 g (0.7 oz) fresh yeast or 2 tsp dry yeast
- Pinch of saffron powder
- 80 g (⅓ cup) butter, room temperature

Egg wash

- 1 egg yolk

METHOD

- In a large bowl, whisk together the flour, sugar and salt. In another bowl, whisk together the milk, yeast and saffron powder.
- Make a well in the flour and add the liquid ingredients. Stir this together until a dough starts to form, then add the butter and knead on a flat surface for about 10 minutes, or until smooth and elastic. Alternatively, mix for about 8 minutes in a stand mixer with a dough hook.
- Cover and let rise for about 1–2 hours or until the dough has doubled in size.
- Shape the dough into one large, round loaf. Let rise again for about 30 minutes (or until you push the surface with your finger and the dough bounces back in place).
- Preheat oven to 200°C/400°F/gas mark 6.
- Brush the dough with the egg yolk, then cut a diagonal grid into the top of the bread.
- Bake for about 40–45 minutes, or until it is golden and it makes a hollow sound when tapped on the bottom.

TIPS

- Saffron is a potent spice and you only need a little to impart color and flavor. If you have saffron threads instead of powder, use a mortar and pestle to grind them before adding.

FRUIT

Fruit in Switzerland is a seasonal affair. The general populace gets excited when the first Swiss strawberries appear in the spring, followed closely by rhubarb, then roadside stands of Valais apricots in the summer, and fresh apple and grape juice in the fall. There are cherries, too, and pears, as well as blackberries, blueberries, currants and all manner of plums.

According to the Swiss Farmer's Union, of the nearly 7000 hectares (17 acres) used to grow fruit, about half of it is used to grow apples. Apples are deeply embedded in Swiss culture, and not just the beautiful trees dotting the landscape. They have been a symbol of the country and its independent spirit ever since William Tell shot the apple off his son's head. Perhaps that's one reason why the Swiss love apples more than any other fruit? The Swiss Fruit Union reports that they eat over 16 kg (35 lbs) per person, per year.

39

BIRCHERMÜESLI

Creamy oats for any time of day

If you're at a hotel breakfast buffet in Switzerland you'll probably see a big bowl of *Birchermüesli*—a creamy mix of oats, yogurt and fruit. Today it's enjoyed in all regions of the country, but the original *Birchermüesli* was created by Dr. Maximilian Oskar Bircher-Benner. It was an integral part of his treatment program for patients at his sanatorium near Zurich.

Müesli means "little mush" in German, and his combination of grated apple, oats, condensed milk, lemon juice, and nuts embodied his ideas about the importance of raw, nutritious food in the treatment of diseases.

Raw foodism, like other food trends, seems to fade in and out of popularity, but Dr. Bircher's muesli is something that has crept into the common culinary pantheon. Although the muesli you find today is a departure from Dr. Bircher's refreshing apple mush, it still hints at his ideas of health and nutrition.

Here are two variations of this beloved Swiss dish—a wholesome version where you can choose your own nuts and fruits, and a quick and easy version from my Aunt Vreni, using packaged muesli.

SERVINGS
4

INGREDIENTS

Wholesome Birchermüesli

- 4 tbsp rolled oats
- 6 tbsp milk
- 2 apples, finely grated
- 2 tbsp raisins (or other dried fruit)
- 2 tbsp chopped nuts
- 300 g (1¼ cups) plain yogurt
- 400–500 g (about 1 lb) seasonal fruit

Aunt Vreni's Birchermüesli

- 140 g (1½ cups) packaged muesli
- About 350–400 g (1½ cups) fruit yogurt
- 125 ml (½ cup) milk
- 400–500 g (about 1 lb) seasonal fruit

METHOD

- Mix everything except the seasonal fruit together in a large bowl.
- Cover and let sit in the fridge for a couple of hours, or overnight.
- Stir in the seasonal fruit and a splash of milk, then serve.

TIPS

- Packaged muesli is usually a mix of oats, raisins, nuts, and other dried fruits. A popular brand outside of Switzerland is Alpen. You could also just use rolled oats and add dried fruit and nuts at will.
- After sitting, the *Birchermüesli* can be a bit stodgy; you can stir in a splash of milk before serving.

CHOLERMÜS

An eggy pancake perfect for compotes

Typically eaten for dinner, this easy, sliced pancake from central Switzerland also makes an excellent breakfast with fruit or even maple syrup. You may know its Alpine relatives—the similar *Tatsch* from Graubünden, as well as *Kaiserschmarrn* from Austria.

SERVINGS
4

INGREDIENTS

- 300 g (2⅓ cups) flour
- ½ tsp salt
- 300 ml (1¼ cups) milk
- 300 ml (1¼ cups) heavy cream
- 6 eggs

METHOD

- In a large bowl, whisk together the flour and salt. In a large measuring cup, whisk together the milk, cream and eggs, then whisk into the flour mixture. Cover and let rest for about 30 minutes.

- In a large frying pan, heat 1 tbsp of the butter. Give the batter a whisk to loosen it up, then pour half into the frying pan. Let cook over medium heat for about 3–5 minutes or until the liquid on top is mostly set and the bottom is golden brown.

- With a flat wooden spoon or similar implement, cut the batter into pieces. As you break up the pieces, move them around the pan to brown on all sides. Remove from the pan and keep warm. Add the remaining tablespoon of butter to the pan and repeat with the remaining batter.

- Serve with warm compote, sliced fruit or cinnamon sugar.

TIPS

- The ingredient that sets this dish apart from its pancake relatives is cream; however, you can reduce this amount and replace it with milk, if desired.

41

CHRIESIAUFLAUF

Semolina pudding with bright, juicy cherries

Switzerland is a cherry paradise, but it's possible that no place loves their *Chriesi* (cherries) more than Zug. Famous for the beautiful trees that dot the landscape, this fruit has been the pride of the canton for centuries. Their famous cherry market was first documented in 1627, and their cherry bell, *Chriesiglogg ä*, in 1711. Once the cherries in Zug's public orchard were ripe, the *Chriesiglogg ä* would ring for half an hour to signal the start of the *Chriesisturm*: the storming of the orchard.

At this point, all the residents had the right to pick the cherries. They would take their ladders, wicker backpacks and cherry-picking tools and dash through the town to get their hands on the first fruit. The tradition of the *Chriesisturm* faded in the 20th century but was reinstated in 2009. Now the streets are once again full of people running with ladders, only this time instead of frantic cherry picking, the participants have a calm, bountiful cherry lunch together in the town square.

One beloved cherry dish is this gratin—juicy cherries at the bottom with a fluffy topping of eggs and semolina—that first appeared in the region in the latter half of the 18th century.

SERVINGS
4

INGREDIENTS

Filling

- 800 g (1¾ lbs) cherries

Batter

- 200 g (1¼ cups) fine semolina
- 250 ml (1 cup) milk
- 120 g (½ cup) plain yogurt
- 80 g (⅓ cup) butter, melted
- 80 g (⅓ cup) sugar
- 3 eggs, separated
- 1 tsp vanilla paste or extract
- Zest of half a lemon

Topping

- 150 g flaked almonds

METHOD

- Preheat oven to 200°C/400°F/gas mark 6.
- Grease a 2.5 liter (10 cup) casserole dish. Pit the cherries and place in the dish.
- In a large bowl, whisk together the semolina, milk, yogurt, melted butter, sugar, egg yolks, vanilla, and zest.
- In a separate bowl, using an electric mixer with a whisk attachment, whip the egg whites until soft peaks form, then fold into the batter.
- Spread the batter over the cherries and bake for about 30 minutes, remove from the oven and sprinkle the almonds over top, then bake for an additional 15 minutes or until the top has browned and the cherries start to bubble through.

TIPS

- More on whipping egg whites on page 16.

42

FRÜCHTEWÄHE – TARTE AUX FRUITS

Perfect for all kinds of seasonal fruit

If you need to feed a crowd, have a glut of fruit, or simply don't feel like faffing with a tart pan, then this is the fruit tart for you!

SERVINGS

6–8

INGREDIENTS

Dough

- 300 g (2⅓ cups) flour
- 3 tbsp sugar
- 1 tsp salt
- 110 g (½ cup) butter, cold
- 180 ml (¾ cup) water, cold

Filling

- 80g (⅔ cup) ground nuts
- 1–1.5 kg (2–3 lbs) fruit (apricots, plums, blueberries, etc.)
- 2 eggs
- 250 ml (1 cup) milk
- 150 ml (⅔ cup) heavy cream
- 2 tbsp sugar
- 1 tsp vanilla paste or extract

METHOD

Dough

- In a large bowl, whisk together the flour, sugar and salt. Add the cold butter in pieces and rub into the flour mixture with your fingers until you have small flakes.

- Make a well in the middle of the flour, add the water and mix gently until a dough forms. Shape the dough into a disc, wrap, and let cool in the fridge for about an hour.

- Line a large baking sheet (about 35 x 40 cm/13 x 18 in) with parchment paper (alternatively, lightly grease the baking sheet), then roll out the dough on top. Poke the bottom of the dough all over lightly with a fork, then keep cool until you have the filling ready.

Filling

- Preheat oven to 200°C/400°F/gas mark 6, bottom heat.

- Whisk together the eggs, milk, cream, sugar, and vanilla. Spread the ground nuts over the dough, then pit and cut the fruit as necessary (halve or quarter the larger fruits like apricots or plums) and arrange on top. Pour over the egg/milk mixture.

- Bake in the bottom half of the oven for about 25–30 minutes, or until the liquid has set and the bottom is baked through.

Continued next page

TIPS

- My favorite fruits to use here are apricots, plums, apples (these are also nice grated), rhubarb, cherries, or blueberries. You can do a mix of different fruits too.

- You can use frozen fruit: just place it directly from the freezer on the tart (no need to defrost). Baking time may increase slightly.

- The exact amount of fruit and egg/milk mixture is variable, based on the size of the fruit, but use as much as fits comfortably onto the pan, making sure the egg/milk mixture doesn't spill over.

43

TARTE AUX PRUNEAUX

A jammy, plum-topped tart

This tart appears in the fall when little prune plums, *pruneaux* in French and *Zwetschge*n in German, have their season. It's linked to the interfaith holiday of *Jeûne fédéral/Bettag*, the federal day of Thanksgiving, Repentance and Prayer celebrated on the third Sunday in September. In Geneva, the holiday is known as *Jeûne genevois* and celebrated the Thursday after the first Sunday in September. These plum tarts were easy to prepare in advance, and after the day of fasting and prayer, they were enjoyed at dinnertime.

SERVINGS

6

INGREDIENTS

Dough

- 200 g (1⅔ cups) flour
- Pinch of salt
- 80 g (⅓ cup) butter, cold

Filling

- About 800 g (1¾ lbs) fresh Pruneaux/Zwetschgen (small prune plums)
- 60 g (½ cup) ground nuts
- 3 tbsp sugar
- 1 tsp cinnamon

METHOD

Dough

- In a large bowl, whisk together the flour, sugar and salt. Add the cold butter in pieces and rub into the flour mixture with your fingers until you have small flakes.
- Make a well in the middle of the flour, add the water and mix gently until a dough forms. Shape the dough into a disc, wrap, and let cool in the fridge for about an hour.
- Roll out the dough and line a 28 cm (11 in) round springform or tart pan. Poke the bottom of the dough all over lightly with a fork, then keep cool until you have the filling ready.

Filling

- Preheat oven to 200°C/400°F/gas mark 6, bottom heat.
- Pit and halve or quarter the plums.
- Place the tart pan on a parchment-lined baking sheet, sprinkle with the nuts, sugar and cinnamon, then arrange the plums in rows on top.
- Bake in the bottom part of the oven for about 40–50 minutes, or until the fruit juices are bubbling.

TIPS

- In French-speaking Switzerland, the filling is typically just plums, or pour over 125 ml (½ cup) heavy cream whisked with 2 tbsp sugar and 1 tsp cornstarch before baking. In the German-speaking part, the filling typically contains eggs: add 125 ml (½ cup) each of milk and heavy cream, whisked with 2 eggs and 3 tbsp sugar before baking.

44

TARTE AUX POIRES À LA GENEVOISE

Geneva's juicy pear tart

This buttery pear and raisin tart is traditionally served during Geneva's *Escalade* celebrations. On the night of December 11–12, 1602, Protestant Geneva was attacked by the Catholic forces of Charles Emmanuel, Duke of Savoy, who ordered his soldiers to climb (*escalade*) the city's battlements with ladders.

Much to their surprise, the citizens, alongside the town's militia, fought back heartily against the sneak attack and defeated the Savoy forces. The hero of the night was an elderly woman known as Mère Royaume, who poured her cauldron of boiling vegetable soup on the head of a Savoyard soldier.

Today, there is still feasting to celebrate this holiday, and the final course is often this tart. It's easy to make—the hardest part is slicing slippery pears—and its buttery crust and juicy filling make it irresistible.

SERVINGS
6

INGREDIENTS

Dough

- 1 package puff pastry dough (about 250 g/½ lb)

Filling

- 150 g (1 cup) raisins
- 2 tbsp Williams (pear *eau-de-vie*)
- 80 ml (⅓ cup) white wine
- About 8 pears, cored and sliced
- 80 ml (⅓ cup) heavy cream
- 4 tbsp sugar
- 80 g (⅔ cup) ground walnuts
- 1 tbsp cinnamon

METHOD

Dough

- Roll out the pastry and line a 26 cm (10 in) springform or tart pan. Poke the bottom of the pastry all over with a fork, then keep cool until you have the filling ready.

Filling

- Preheat oven to 200°C/400°F/gas mark 6, bottom heat.

- In a medium bowl, mix together the raisins, Williams and wine and let soak. In a separate bowl, mix together the sliced pears, cream and 2 tbsp of the sugar. Sprinkle the puff pastry base with the ground walnuts, the remaining 2 tbsp sugar and cinnamon, then add the pears and raisins.

- Bake in the bottom half of the oven for about 30 minutes or until the dough comes away from the side and the pear mixture is bubbling.

TIPS

- I typically leave the skin on the pears when making this tart, because I like the texture it gives, but you can also peel them first.

- If you don't have Williams or another fruit eau-de-vie, just substitute with more white wine.

45

THURGAUER ÖPFELTORTE

Easy apple cake

This wonderful cake comes from Thurgau, Switzerland's premier apple region—one that boasts apple museums, apple-themed hiking trails, apple blossom spa visits, and even a pageant that crowns the yearly *Apfelkönigin* (apple queen).

SERVINGS

6

INGREDIENTS

- 180 g (¾ cup) butter
- 150 g (¾ cup) sugar
- 3 eggs
- ½ tsp salt
- Zest and juice of half a lemon
- 300 g (2⅓ cups) flour
- 1 tsp baking powder
- 4–5 medium apples
- 1 tbsp sugar
- 1 tsp cinnamon

METHOD

- Preheat oven to 180°C/350°F/gas mark 4.
- Line the bottom of a 26 cm (10 in) springform pan with parchment paper and grease the sides. Set aside.
- In a large bowl, beat together the butter and sugar for 2–3 minutes, or until pale and fluffy, then beat in the eggs, salt, and lemon zest and juice. Add the flour and baking powder, and mix until combined, then spread into the buttered pan.
- Peel, core and slice the apples (you can do this like in the photo, or simply cut them in slices), then arrange on top of the batter.
- Mix together the cinnamon and sugar, then sprinkle over the cake. Bake for about 30–35 minutes, or until the apples start to brown slightly and the cake pulls away from the sides of the pan and springs back under your finger when pressed.

TIPS

- You can use most firm apples, like Braeburn, Gala, Jazz, or Pink Lady.

46

HOIBEERISTURM

A blueberry "storm" with sweet, roasted breadcrumbs and cream

Hoibeeri is one of the Swiss German dialect words for blueberry, and where I live in the Emmental they can be eaten as a *Sturm* (storm)—cooked, mixed with cream, and topped with toasted bread. Don't have blueberries? No problem! You can make your *Sturm* with raspberries, blackberries or even cherries, and it works well with frozen fruit too.

SERVINGS
4

INGREDIENTS

- 1 tbsp of butter
- 4 tbsp sugar
- 300 g (4 cups) leftover bread, cubed
- 500 g (1 lb) blueberries
- 80 ml (⅓ cup) heavy cream
- 1 tsp of vanilla paste or extract

METHOD

- In a medium frying pan, heat the butter then sprinkle in 2 tbsp of the sugar. Over medium heat, let the sugar dissolve and start to melt, then add the cubed bread and keep stirring, until toasted, for about 5 minutes. Remove the bread from the pan and set aside.

- Add the blueberries and remaining 2 tbsp of sugar to the frying pan and cook for a few minutes, or until they begin to break down. Stir in the cream and vanilla and take off the heat. Have a quick taste for sweetness, and if the berries are too tart, add a bit more sugar. Spoon into bowls, topping with the toasted bread.

TIPS

- A great way to use up leftover *Zopf*.
- You can use fresh or frozen fruit; frozen will just take slightly longer to cook.

COZY CAKES

With a cup of milky coffee in hand, the following cakes are perfect for sharing with your loved ones. Whereas the previous chapter included all the best fruit-filled and -topped cakes, this chapter includes cozy cakes that are simple to make year-round.

You'll find *Rüeblitorte*, a nutty carrot cake from Aargau, and *Tuorta da Nusch*, a caramel and walnut tart from Graubünden. There's *Lebkuchen*, a kind of gingerbread (this version from the canton of Lucerne), and a wonderful cake from Ticino, *Torta di Pane*, meant to help use up leftover bread. Speaking of bread, there's *Salée au Sucre*, a delicious cake involving a yeasted base and a simple topping of cream and sugar. The *St. Galler Klostertorte* was founded in Switzerland's most famous monastery, and there's even the *Glarner Pastete* from Glarus with two fillings in one cake, for when you just can't make up your mind.

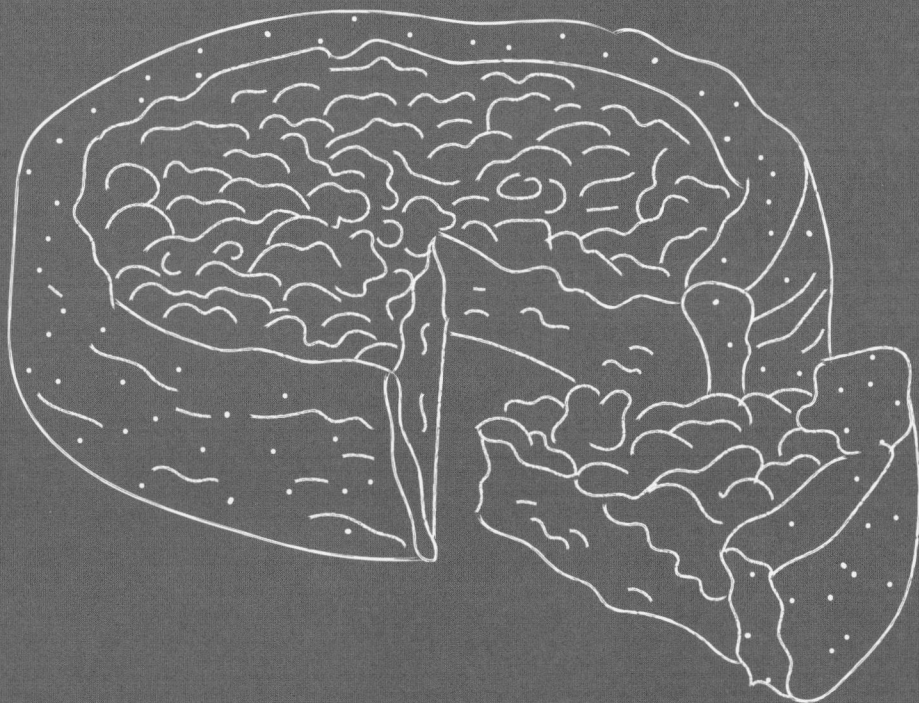

47

RÜEBLITORTE

Nutty carrot cake

This carrot cake comes from the canton of Aargau, one of the major producers of Swiss carrots, and fondly known as *Rüebliland* (carrot country). The city of Aarau also boasts a yearly *Rüeblimärt* (carrot market) every first Wednesday of November.

SERVINGS
8

INGREDIENTS

- 250 g (½ lb) carrots, peeled and finely grated
- 300 g (2½ cups) ground hazelnuts
- 75 g (⅔ cup) flour
- 1 tsp baking powder
- Pinch of salt
- 4 eggs, separated
- 275 g (1⅓ cups) sugar
- 1 tbsp kirsch
- Icing sugar, to decorate

METHOD

- Preheat oven to 180°C/350°F/gas mark 4.
- Line the bottom of a 24 cm (9 in) springform pan with parchment paper and grease the sides.
- In a medium bowl, whisk together the ground nuts, flour, baking powder, and salt.
- In a large bowl, whisk the egg yolks and sugar until you get a pale, yellow paste. Add the kirsch and whisk well.
- In a medium bowl, using an electric mixer with a whisk attachment, whip the egg whites until soft peaks form.
- Mix the carrots into the yolk and sugar paste, then fold in the dry ingredients. Finally, gently fold in the beaten egg whites. Spread the batter into the pan.
- Bake for 55–60 minutes, or until the sides come away from the pan and the top springs back when pressed.
- When the cake has cooled completely, dust with icing sugar.

TIPS

- If you don't have hazelnuts, you can substitute with ground almonds.
- More on whipping egg whites on page 16.

48

FABIANA'S LUZERNER LEBKUCHEN

Spice cake from Lucerne

My husband grew up deep in the Entlebuch eating his neighbor Fabiana's delicious gingerbread cake—*Lebkuchen*.

SERVINGS

8

INGREDIENTS

Batter

- 500 g (4 cups) flour
- 250 g (1¼ cups) sugar
- 1 tbsp *Lebkuchen* spice mix
- ½ tsp salt
- 300 ml (1¼ cups) milk
- 300 ml (1¼ cups) heavy cream
- 3 tbsp *Birnenhonig* or honey
- 60 ml (¼ cup) strong coffee
- 1 tsp baking soda
- 2 tsp warm water

Glaze

- 3 tbsp *Birnenhonig* or honey

METHOD

- Preheat oven to 190°C/375°F/gas mark 5.
- Line a 26 cm (10 in) springform pan with parchment paper.
- In a large bowl, whisk together the flour, sugar, *Lebkuchen* spice mix, and salt.
- In a large measuring cup, whisk together the milk and cream. In a small bowl, dissolve the *Birnenhonig* into the coffee and whisk this into the milk mixture.
- Make a well in the middle of the flour mixture and add the milk mixture. Using a spatula, stir gently until almost combined.
- In a small bowl, dissolve the baking soda in the warm water, then add to the batter and stir in gently. Be careful not to over-mix or the cake will become rubbery.
- Spread into the pan and bake for about 50 minutes, or until the sides come away from the pan and the top springs back completely when pressed.
- While the cake is still warm, drizzle the *Birnenhonig* over the top and spread with the back of a spoon.

TIPS

- If you don't have *Lebkuchen* spice mix, mixed spice or gingerbread spice can be used. Or make your own: 5 tbsp cinnamon, 3 tsp cloves, 3 tsp ginger, and 1 tsp each allspice, cardamom, star anise, nutmeg, allspice, and mace. This makes more than required for the recipe: you can store it in an airtight jar for up to a year.
- *Birnenhonig* is a syrup made from pears. You can substitute it with honey, treacle or molasses.

49

TUORTA DA NUSCH

A buttery crust bursting with caramel walnuts

Tuorta da Nusch, or *Engadiner Nusstorte*, is one of Graubünden's most popular cakes and, due to its long shelf life, often bought by tourists to take home. It consists of a thick, buttery crust encasing a caramelly, walnut filling.

SERVINGS

8

INGREDIENTS

Dough

- 300 g (2⅓ cups) flour
- 100 g (½ cup) sugar
- Pinch of salt
- 150 g (⅔ cup) butter, cold
- 1 egg

Filling

- 100 g (⅓ cup) honey
- 250 ml (1 cup) heavy cream
- 250 g (1¼ cups) sugar
- 300 g (3 cups) walnuts, roughly chopped
- ½ tsp salt

Egg wash

- 1 egg, lightly beaten

METHOD

Dough

- In a large bowl, whisk together the flour, sugar and salt. Add the cold butter in pieces and rub into the flour mixture with your fingers until you have small flakes.
- Make a well in the middle of the flour, add the egg, and mix gently until a dough forms. Shape the dough into a disc, wrap, and let cool in the fridge for about an hour.

Filling

- In a small pot, warm the cream and honey until the honey has melted into the cream.
- In a large pot, add the sugar and give it a shake so it covers the bottom in an even layer. Cook over high heat until it liquefies and then turns golden, stirring or swirling a little to keep it cooking evenly. Once it's a light caramel color, add the cream and honey mixture and remove from the heat (careful, it will sputter and seize up), stirring until incorporated. Then stir in the walnuts and salt. Let cool for about 10 minutes.
- Preheat oven to 200°C/400°F/gas mark 6.
- Roll out the dough and line a 26 cm (10 in) springform or tart pan, using about two-thirds for the base and sides. Roll the rest into a 26 cm (10 in) circle—this will be the lid.
- Spread the cooled nut mixture over the dough. Prick the lid all over with a fork, then lay it on top of the tart and press around the edge to seal. Brush with egg wash.
- Bake for about 40 minutes, or until the top is golden brown.

50

TORTA DI PANE

Spiced bread pudding cake from Ticino

Who knew leftover bread could taste this good? This classic bread pudding cake from Ticino has as many versions as there are *nonnas* in the canton. Like other inherited recipes, every household has their own take on what makes it best. Historically, it was baked in Ticino's communal ovens and served at local festivals.

SERVINGS
8

INGREDIENTS

Bread mixture

- 750 ml (3 cups) milk
- 1 tsp vanilla paste or extract
- ½ tsp salt
- 300 g (4 cups) leftover bread, cubed
- 100 g (1 cup) amaretti or other cookies, crushed

Filling

- 200 g (1½ cups) raisins
- Grappa or warm black tea
- Zest and juice of 1 orange
- 2 tsp cinnamon
- ½ tsp each of cloves, nutmeg
- 2 tbsp cocoa powder
- 60 g (2 oz) dark chocolate, chopped
- 80 g (⅔ cup) ground almonds

Batter

- 100 g (½ cup) sugar
- 2 eggs

Topping

- 100 g (⅔ cup) pine nuts

METHOD

Bread mixture

- In a large pot, bring the milk, vanilla and salt to a simmer, then remove from heat. Add the cubed bread and cookies. Cover and let sit for about an hour.

Filling

- Place the raisins in a bowl and cover with grappa or tea. Set aside.
- Grease a 26 cm (10 in) springform pan and line the bottom with parchment paper.
- Preheat oven to 180°C/350°F/gas mark 4.
- Mush together the milky bread mixture with a fork. Add the soaked raisins with two tablespoons of the grappa or tea, orange zest and juice, spices, cocoa powder, dark chocolate, and ground almonds.

Batter

- In a medium bowl, whisk together the eggs and sugar. Gently stir this into the bread mixture, then spread into the prepared pan and sprinkle the edge with pine nuts.
- Bake for about an hour, or until the cake has set and the top looks dry.

GLARNER PASTETE

Two fillings for the price of one

Half filled with plum paste and half with almond paste, this flaky tart from Glarus is made in numerous bakeries throughout the region, and sometimes in celebration of the canton's patron saint, Fridolin. Little individual versions of the tart are called *Beggeli* and filled with either plums or almonds.

SERVINGS
8

INGREDIENTS

Plum filling

- 150 g (¾ cup) prunes
- 250 ml (1 cup) brewed black tea, still hot
- 1 tbsp kirsch
- 1 tsp cinnamon

Almond filling

- 100 g (¾ cup) ground almonds
- 3 tbsp sugar
- Zest and juice of half a lemon
- 1 tsp cinnamon

Assembly

- 500 g (1 lb) puff pastry
- Icing sugar

METHOD

Plum filling

- Place the dried plums in a bowl, cover with tea, and let steep for about 30 minutes.
- Drain the plums, reserving the tea liquid. Add the kirsch and cinnamon to the plums and, using an immersion blender or food processor, make a paste. If it seems too thick (it should be spreadable), add some of the reserved tea, a tablespoon at a time.

Almond filling

- Mix together the almonds, sugar, lemon zest and juice, cinnamon, and 2 tbsp of the reserved tea from the steeped plums. It should be moist and spreadable, but if it seems thick, just add some more reserved tea liquid.

Assembly

- Preheat oven to 200°C/400°F/gas mark 6.
- Roll out half of the puff pastry and place on a parchment-lined baking sheet. Fold in the edge 2 cm (1 in) to create a rim all the way around.
- Spread plum filling on one half of the base and almond on the other. Roll out the second half of the puff pastry and also fold in the edge 2 cm (1 in) to create a rim. Place the pastry lid on top and press gently around the edge. The traditional shape is like a large flower, which you can make by cutting eight even petals. You can also leave it round. Cut eight slashes into the dough, pointing from the middle toward the edge.
- Bake for about 30–35 minutes, or until the top and bottom are golden. Let cool, then dust with icing sugar.

52

SALÉE AU SUCRE

Simple, but satisfying, bread with sugar and cream

If you're looking for unassuming yet impossibly delicious baked goods, look no further than Switzerland's suite of yeast-raised doughs topped with cream and sugar. In the villages at the base of Mount Vully in the canton of Fribourg, you'll find the *Gâteau de Vully* which is known as the *Disque d'Or* (golden disc). Across the lake in the picturesque town of Murten, they sell *Nidelkuchen* (cream cake), which you'll also find in the canton of Bern.

Salée au Sucre is another version especially beloved in canton Vaud and made cake-sized or sometimes smaller; about the size of your hand. Don't let the name fool you—although *salée* means salty in French, in the olden days it simply was another word for "cake."

SERVINGS
8

INGREDIENTS

Dough

- 300 g (2⅓ cups) flour
- 1 tbsp sugar
- 1 tsp salt
- 180 ml (¾ cup) milk, room temperature
- 20 g (0.7 oz) fresh yeast or 2 tsp dry yeast
- 2 tbsp butter, room temperature

Topping

- 150 ml (⅔ cup) heavy cream
- 120 g (½ cup) crème fraîche
- 100 g (½ cup) sugar

Egg wash

- 1 egg yolk

METHOD

Dough

- In a large bowl, whisk together the flour and salt. In another bowl, whisk together the milk, sugar and yeast.

- Make a well in the flour and add the liquid ingredients. Stir this together until a dough starts to form, then add the butter and knead on a flat surface for about 10–15 minutes, or until smooth and elastic. Alternatively, mix for about 10 minutes in a stand mixer with a dough hook. Cover and let rise for about an hour or until the dough has doubled in size.

- Line the bottom of a 26 cm (11 in) springform pan with parchment paper and grease the sides. Roll out the dough into a circle, and place into the pan, gently stretching it to the edge. Let rest for about 30 minutes.

Topping

- Preheat oven to 190°C/375°F/gas mark 5.

- In a measuring cup, whisk together the topping ingredients.

- Press the dough down so it has a slightly raised edge, then top with half the cream mixture. Brush the edge with the egg wash. Bake for 15 minutes.

- Take the cake out of the oven, pour over the remaining topping cream, then bake for another 15 minutes or until the top is set and starting to brown.

- Take out of the oven, remove the sides of the springform and let the cake cool fully.

53

ST. GALLER KLOSTERTORTE

A thick, nutty crust with tangy jam shining through

A close cousin of Austria's famous *Linzertorte*, this one is made Swiss by adding, of course, chocolate. The torte comes from the *Kloster* (monastery) of St. Gallen. Although a written version of the *Klostertorte* didn't appear until 1947 when the abbey was no longer in use, it is probable that some version of it had been made in the monastery bakehouses.

SERVINGS

8

INGREDIENTS

Dough

- 200 g (¾ cup + 2 tbsp) butter, room temperature
- 150 g (¾ cup) sugar
- 2 eggs, room temperature
- Pinch of salt
- 200 g (1⅔ cups) flour
- 100 g (¾ cup) ground almonds
- 80 g (⅔ cup) cocoa powder
- 1 tsp baking powder
- 1 tsp cinnamon

Filling

- 400 g (1¼ cups) raspberry jam

METHOD

- Line the bottom of a 28 cm (11 in) round springform or tart pan with parchment paper.
- In a large bowl, beat together the butter and sugar for 2–3 minutes, or until pale and fluffy, then beat in the eggs and salt.
- In a separate bowl, whisk together the flour, nuts, cocoa powder, baking powder, and cinnamon. Add to the butter mixture and mix until just combined.
- Shape the dough into a disc, wrap with plastic, and let cool in the fridge for about an hour.
- Preheat oven to 180°C/350°F/gas mark 4.
- Using a little flour, roll out two thirds of the dough into a 28 cm (11 in) round. Place on the bottom of the prepared pan. If there are cracks anywhere, lightly press in some extra dough. Spread the jam over the base, leaving about a 1 cm (½ in) edge free.
- Roll out the remaining dough to make the top. It could have a lattice design, or sometimes forms are simply cut out with small cookie cutters and arranged at will.
- Bake for about 30–35 minutes, or until the jam is bubbling.

COOKIES

The Swiss are wild about cookies, especially during the Christmas season.

In December, when days are cold and there's little sunlight, Swiss families often gather together to bake cookies. It's an important feature of Advent—the run up to Christmas—with some families making over a dozen different varieties. The most beloved Christmas recipes are dusted off, a schedule is made, recipes are double-checked, and maybe a new one is added into the rotation.

Ingredients are prepared—chilled, toasted, warmed, ground—and tools and tins are brought forth, as well as promises from family members to help with certain parts of the baking day(s). Each variety of cookie is carefully stacked in its own tin, and when guests come to call, or you are invited to someone's house, a plate is arranged with the many cookies on display.

The cookies in this book include some of the most popular Christmas cookies, as well as the light and airy meringue, a perfect partner to rich Swiss cream.

54

MAILÄNDERLI – MILANAIS

Switzerland's favorite Christmas cookie

Mailänderli, known as *Milanais* in French and *Milanese* in Italian, are the standard Swiss Christmas cookie made by nearly every bakery and every family in the country. Buttery with a hint of lemon, the taste is a nostalgic reminder of childhood and Christmas for many Swiss people living at home or abroad.

In the 19th century, the cookies featured at New Year's parties in Basel. The Baslers called them *Gaatoodemylängli*, from the French *gâteaux de Milan*, and served them with their famous mulled wine, *Hypokras*.

MAKES
About 30

INGREDIENTS

Dough

- 125 g (½ cup) butter, room temperature
- 125 g (½ cup) sugar
- 3 egg yolks (55 g/2 oz)
- Zest of 1 lemon
- Pinch of salt
- 250 g (2 cups) flour

Glaze

- 1 egg yolk
- Pinch of sugar

METHOD

- In a large bowl, beat together the butter and sugar for 2–3 minutes, or until pale and fluffy, then beat in the three egg yolks one at a time.
- Add the lemon zest and salt. Add the flour and mix until combined. Form the dough into two discs, wrap, and chill in the fridge for about an hour, or until firm.
- Using a little flour, roll out the dough to about 0.7–1 cm (¼–½ in) thick. Cut out the cookies with 3–4 cm (1–2 in) cutters and place on parchment-lined baking sheets. For best results, chill again in the fridge for about an hour, or the freezer for about 15 minutes.
- Preheat oven to 180°C/350°F/gas mark 4.
- Whisk together the egg yolk and sugar and brush an even layer on the cookies. Bake for about 10–12 minutes, or until the glaze is set and the bottoms are golden.

TIPS

- If the dough looks dry once you've mixed in the flour, add a little more yolk or milk.
- Using just yolks makes for a beautifully rich and golden dough, but you can swap out the three yolks for one whole egg, if desired.
- Stored in tins, the cookies keep for about a week.

55

BASLER BRUNSLI

Elegant chocolate and nut cookies

You'll find these nutty, chocolate beauties on Christmas cookie platters throughout the country. Originating in the city of Basel, they were initially baked not only at Christmas, but also for weddings and other special occasions.

MAKES
About 60

INGREDIENTS

Dough

- 200 g (1⅔ cups) ground hazelnuts or almonds
- 200 g (1 cup) sugar, plus more for sprinkling
- 100 g (3½ oz) dark chocolate, finely grated
- 80 g (1 cup) cocoa powder
- 2 tsp cinnamon
- 1 tsp salt
- 3 egg whites (105 g/3½ oz)
- 2 tsp kirsch

METHOD

- In a large bowl, whisk together the nuts, sugar, chocolate, cocoa powder, cinnamon, and salt.
- In a separate large bowl, using an electric mixer with a whisk attachment, whip the egg whites until soft peaks form. Fold in the dry ingredients and kirsch.
- Form into two discs, wrap, and chill in the fridge for about an hour, or until firm.
- Preheat oven to 200°C/400°F/gas mark 6.
- Sprinkle sugar onto a flat surface (instead of flour) and roll out the dough to about 0.7–1 cm (¼–½ in) thick, then cut out with 4–5 cm (1½–2 in) cutters and place on a parchment-lined baking sheet.
- Bake the cookies for about 8 minutes, or until you can smell them and their tops look dry.

TIPS

- More on whipping egg whites on page 16.
- Stored in tins, the cookies keep for up to two weeks.

56

SPITZBUBEN — MIROIRS

Cheeky peek-a-boo jam cookies

These cookies, known as *Miroirs* in French and *Discoletti* in Italian, can be sandwiched with your jam of choice—favorites being raspberry, currant or quince. The Swiss-German name *Spitzbub* refers to a mischievous boy, and the cookies were so named because of the jammy faces cut into the dough.

MAKES

About 30

INGREDIENTS

Dough

- 170 g (¾ cup) butter, room temperature
- 150 g (¾ cup) sugar
- 1 egg
- 1 tsp vanilla paste or extract
- 1 tsp salt
- 300 g (2⅓ cups) flour

Assembly

- 150 g (½ cup) jam
- Icing sugar

METHOD

- In a large bowl, beat together the butter and sugar for about 2–3 minutes, or until pale and fluffy, then beat in the egg, vanilla and salt. Add the flour and mix until combined. Form into a disc, wrap, and chill in the fridge for an hour, or until firm.
- Preheat oven to 180°C/350°F/gas mark 4.
- Using a little flour, roll out the dough to ½ cm (⅕ in) thick and cut out cookies 5–7 cm (2–3 in) in diameter, trying not to work the dough too much when you re-roll.
- Place on a parchment-lined baking sheet, then use a small cookie cutter or paring knife to cut an additional hole (or smiley face) in half of the cookies to make the tops.
- Bake for 10–12 minutes, or until just golden.
- Dust icing sugar over the tops. Sandwich about a teaspoon of jam between a top and bottom cookie, pressing together until the jam peeks out the hole.

TIPS

- If the jam is very thick, you can give it is good stir before sandwiching it, or warm it slightly.
- Stored in tins, the assembled cookies keep for about a week. Because of the jam, these cookies will naturally soften. If you prefer a crispier cookie, you can store the halves and assemble when needed.

57

TOTENBEINLI

Crunchy cookies bursting with nuts

Totenbeinli, meaning "bones of the dead," are crunchy, nutty cookies originating from Graubünden. This macabre name comes from the fact that they were once commonly served at wakes, and should be about as hard and crunchy as the aforementioned bones.

Today they are made year-round throughout the country, and under much more neutral names like *Nussstängeli* (nut sticks) in German and *croquants* in French, describing their crunchiness.

MAKES
About 34

INGREDIENTS

Nuts

- 150 g (1 cup) whole almonds or hazelnuts
- 120 g (1 cup) ground almonds or hazelnuts

Dough

- 100 g (½ cup) butter, room temperature
- 200 g (1 cup) sugar
- 2 eggs
- ½ tsp salt
- 180 g (1½ cups) flour
- 1 tsp baking powder
- 1 tsp cinnamon

METHOD

Nuts

- Spread the whole and ground nuts on a baking sheet and toast in an oven heated to 180°C/350°F/gas mark 4 for about 6–7 minutes or until lightly browned. Alternatively, you can toast them in batches in a frying pan, over medium heat.

- Let cool completely, then roughly chop up about half of the whole nuts. You will have three kinds of nuts to add: ground, roughly chopped and whole.

Dough

- In a large bowl, beat together the butter and sugar for 2–3 minutes, or until pale and fluffy, then beat in the eggs and salt. In a separate bowl, whisk together the flour, baking powder and cinnamon, then mix into the butter mixture. Fold in the nuts.

- The dough will be quite soft, so use an offset spatula to spread into a flat loaf directly on a parchment-lined baking sheet measuring about 30 x 15 x 1 cm (11 x 6 x ½ in). Chill in the fridge for about an hour, or freezer for about 15 minutes, until firm.

Continued on next page

- Preheat oven to 200°C/400°F/gas mark 6.
- Bake for about 20–25 minutes or until the top has completely set.
- Remove from the oven and wait about 5 minutes, or until cool enough to handle. Cut into long slices, place back on the baking sheet and bake for an additional 6–8 minutes, or until they're just starting to brown around the edges.

TIPS

- Stored in tins, the cookies keep for up to two weeks.

58

MERINGUE

Light, crispy and perfectly paired with thick whipped cream

There are many places in Switzerland where you can eat meringues: those crisp, light confections made from whipped egg whites and sugar.

Here in the Emmental, we eat the meringues (or *Merängge* in local dialect) from Kemmeriboden-Bad with loads of whipped cream or as part of an ice cream sundae. In Gruyères in the canton of Fribourg, they are served with little barrels of thick double cream.

But it's Meiringen, in the Bernese Alps, that claims to be the birthplace of the meringue. The story goes that Gasparini, an Italian chef, invented the delicacy and named it after the town where he worked.

MAKES

About 8

INGREDIENTS

- 4 egg whites (120–130 g/ 4–4½ oz), room temperature
- 200 g (1 cup) sugar
- 1 tsp vanilla paste or vanilla extract

METHOD

- Preheat oven to 100°C/200°F/gas mark 1.
- Using a large bowl and an electric mixer with a whisk attachment, whip the egg whites until they begin to get foamy. Add a tablespoon of sugar and beat in. About every 10 seconds, add a heaping tablespoon of sugar and repeat until it is all beaten in and the mixture is firming up. Add the vanilla.
- Continue beating until the egg whites are stiff and glossy.
- Transfer the mixture into a piping bag. Pipe 8 meringues onto a baking sheet.
- Place the baking sheet in the oven. Use a wooden spoon to prop open the oven door, leaving a gap to let any moisture escape. Bake for about 2 hours, then turn off the heat and let dry out for an additional few hours in the oven.

TIPS

- More on whipping egg whites on page 16.
- Stored in a tin, the meringues keep for about a week.

CHOCOLATE

If you're a chocolate lover, Switzerland is the place for you!

Switzerland has been producing chocolate since the 17th century and revolutionized chocolate production in two ways.

In 1875, Daniel Peter made milk chocolate using powdered milk, and in 1879 Rodolphe Lindt invented the conching process, which pressed the gritty chocolate of the time into the smooth mass we know today.

A boom followed, with numerous new chocolate companies opening up in the early 20th century. Although some of the smaller companies have now been bought up by huge conglomerates, there are still many independent Swiss chocolate factories that have been operating for more than a century.

Today, the chocolate industry in Switzerland is still booming, with the Swiss themselves consuming the highest proportion of chocolate worldwide per capita. According to Chocosuisse, the organization of Swiss chocolate producers, the average Swiss person ate 10.9 kg (24 lbs) of chocolate in 2023.

59

CARAC

An eye-catching tart with a thick chocolate center

A magnet for children (and my husband), the bright green icing hides an intense chocolate filling. They are typically sold as individual tarts, but you can save yourself the trouble of making lots of little ones by making a big tart and serving thin slices.

SERVINGS

8–10

INGREDIENTS

Dough

- 150 g (1 cup + 1 tbsp) flour
- 60 g (½ cup) ground almonds
- 80 g (⅓ cup) sugar
- ½ tsp salt
- 100 g (½ cup) butter, cold
- 1 egg, lightly whisked

Filling

- 125 ml (½ cup) heavy cream
- 200 g (7 oz) chocolate, finely chopped

Icing

- 200 g (1⅔ cups) icing sugar
- 2 tbsp water
- Green food coloring (or blue and yellow)

METHOD

- In a large bowl, whisk together the flour, almonds, sugar, and salt. Add the cold butter in pieces and rub into the flour mixture with your fingers until you have small flakes.
- Make a well in the middle of the flour, add the egg and mix gently until a dough forms. Shape the dough into a disc, wrap, and let cool in the fridge for about an hour.
- Roll out the dough to about 1 cm (½ in) thick and place in a 26 cm (10 in) tart pan.
- Preheat oven to 200°C/400°F/gas mark 6.
- Blind bake the crust: Line the tart with parchment paper and fill with pie weights or dried beans. Bake for about 20 minutes, then remove the weights and bake for 15 minutes more. Set aside.

Filling

- Put the chopped chocolate in a large bowl. In a medium pot, over medium heat, warm the cream until hot and simmering, but not boiling. Pour the cream over the chocolate and let sit for about 5 minutes. Whisk the cream and chocolate together until glossy. Carefully pour into the tart shell until about two thirds full. Let cool completely.

Icing

- In a medium bowl, whisk together the icing sugar and water. Add the food coloring until you get your desired shade of green. Gently cover the tarts with green icing, then let set completely. If desired, pipe a dot in the center using melted chocolate.

60

GROSI'S SCHOKOLADECREME

Thick chocolate cream

This chocolate cream, a recipe my grandmother passed down to my mother, is the dessert I most remember from childhood, and one that graced the table after almost every special meal.

SERVINGS

4

INGREDIENTS

- 2 tsp cornstarch
- 2 eggs
- 500 ml (2 cups) milk
- 50 g (¼ cup) sugar
- 100 g (3½ oz) dark chocolate, chopped
- ½ tsp salt

Garnish

- 150 ml (⅔ cup) heavy cream
- Chopped chocolate

METHOD

- In a large bowl, sift the cornstarch into 2 tbsp of the milk. Whisk until it is all dissolved, then whisk in the eggs and set aside.
- In a medium pot over medium heat, add the remaining milk and the sugar. Just before it begins to boil, take the pot off the heat and whisk in the chocolate and salt. Keep whisking until all the chocolate has melted.
- Very slowly pour half of the hot chocolate mixture into the egg mixture, whisking constantly. (This tempers the egg mixture so you can add it to the hot liquid without the eggs curdling.)
- Pour the tempered egg mixture back into the pot and continue whisking over low heat for about 3–4 minutes, or until it has thickened, then pour it through a sieve into a bowl.
- Let cool until no longer hot to the touch, then cover (press plastic wrap directly onto the surface of the cream so it doesn't form a skin) and let cool completely in the fridge for about 3–4 hours.
- Before serving, whip the cream until soft peaks form, then fold into the chocolate mixture. Garnish with some additional chopped chocolate.

TIPS

- Use a (Swiss) dark chocolate that you would like to eat. I like bars with about 70% cocoa content.

61

MOUSSE AU CHOCOLAT À L'ABSINTHE

Light chocolate mousse gets a visit from "The Green Fairy"

Nobody does chocolate better than the Swiss (don't come for me, Belgians!) and one of the simplest desserts is the classic chocolate mousse. Make it even more refined by adding absinthe, an anise-flavored spirit from the Val-de-Travers in the canton of Neuchâtel.

SERVINGS

4

INGREDIENTS

- 200 g (7 oz) dark chocolate, chopped
- 3 egg whites
- 250 ml (1 cup) heavy cream
- 2 tbsp absinthe

METHOD

- First, melt the chocolate in a microwave or bain-marie. For the bain-marie, put a large pot of water over high heat and set a large bowl on top of it (stainless steel works best). Once the water is boiling, turn off the heat, then add the chocolate to the bowl on top. This should melt with the residual heat, but if it's taking too long, briefly turn the heat back on to low.

- Using an electric mixer with a whisk attachment, whip the egg whites until soft peaks form. Once the chocolate has cooled but is still liquid, whisk in one third of the whipped egg whites and the absinthe. Gently fold in the other two thirds with a spatula.

- In the same bowl you used to whip the whites, pour in the cream and whip it until soft peaks form. On high speed this should take about a minute, but be careful not to over-whip or the mousse will be grainy.

- Fold in the cream then cover and chill in the fridge for at least 2 hours before serving.

TIPS

- If you are concerned about the raw egg whites in this recipe, use pasteurized egg whites.

- More on whipping egg whites on page 16.

- Use a (Swiss) dark chocolate that you would like to eat. I like bars with about 70% cocoa content.

- Don't have absinthe? No problem! You can use another flavorful spirit, like Grand Marnier or dark rum, or just leave it out completely.

DRINKS

Although they have a reputation as mild-mannered and well-ordered, the Swiss do love to drink. They are consistently in the top ten (per capita) of worldwide wine-drinking countries, and they infuse their spirits with everything from hay to their beloved furry edelweiss. Their long history of brewing beer started centuries ago in monasteries, and their much-loved Alpine herbs have been steeped in bottles of bitters and used medicinally to treat things like indigestion for over a hundred years.

Switzerland has plenty of non-alcoholic drinks, too. They are one of the largest exporters of coffee, in the form of Nespresso capsules and Nescafé, and their happy cows arguably produce the world's best milk. The orchards that dot the countryside provide apples for ciders, hard and soft, loved by adults and children, respectively. The fruit trees also produce the base for Switzerland's most famous spirit, kirsch (cherry *eau-de-vie*), as well as numerous other spirits made from pears, apricots and plums.

62

HEISSI SCHOGGI – CHOCOLAT CHAUD

Creamy liquid chocolate

One of the best ways to consume Swiss chocolate is in drinkable form. Here are two recipes: one using chopped chocolate and one with cocoa powder.

For best results use the best quality (Swiss) chocolate you can find. The higher the fat content of the milk, the creamier the hot chocolate will be.

And if you're in a pinch, just pop three Lindt chocolate balls in a mug, fill with hot milk and stir well.

CLASSIC HOT CHOCOLATE
Serves 1

INGREDIENTS

- 250 ml (1 cup) milk
- 30 g (1 oz) dark chocolate, finely chopped
- 20 g (0.7 oz) milk chocolate, finely chopped
- Pinch of salt

METHOD

- In a small pot over medium heat, warm the milk until simmering (make sure it doesn't boil). Remove the pot from the heat and whisk in the chocolate and salt. The chocolate should dissolve, but if you see any lumps, briefly place it back over low heat.

QUICK COCOA
Serves 1

INGREDIENTS

- 250 ml (1 cup) milk
- 1 tbsp unsweetened cocoa powder
- 2 tsp sugar
- 1 tsp of vanilla paste or extract
- Pinch of salt

METHOD

- Whisk everything together in a small pot. Warm over medium heat, but don't boil.

63

VIN CHAUD – GLÜHWEIN

Warm spiced wines, straight from the Christmas markets

If you find yourself at winter events in Switzerland, you're bound to encounter sweet, spiced mulled wine. Here are two versions—white and red. The best white wines to use are slightly sweet, like Gewürztraminer or Pinot Gris, while the best red wines include Pinot Noir, Merlot and the Swiss blend Dôle.

VIN BLANC CHAUD
Serves 4

INGREDIENTS

- 1 bottle of white wine (750 ml)
- 2 cinnamon sticks
- 3 star anise
- 2 oranges, sliced into rounds
- 2 lemons, sliced into rounds
- 50 g (¼ cup) honey

METHOD

- Put everything in a pot and warm over medium heat for about 20 minutes, making sure it doesn't boil.

- Before serving, have a quick taste—if it isn't sweet enough, add a tablespoon more honey, or a squeeze of orange juice (this will very much depend on the sweetness of the wine and your personal preference). Remove the spices before serving.

GLÜHWEIN
Serves 4

INGREDIENTS

- 2 black tea bags
- 1 cinnamon stick
- 3 cloves
- 1 bottle of red wine (750 ml)
- 50 g (¼ cup) sugar
- About 50 ml (¼ cup) brandy or rum
- 2 oranges, sliced into rounds
- 1 lemon, sliced into rounds

METHOD

- Fill a large pot with about 250 ml (1 cup) water. Add the tea bags and spices, bring to a boil, then remove the tea bags. Add the red wine and turn down the temperature to low. Add the sugar, brandy and citrus slices, and simmer on low for about 20 minutes.

- Before serving, have a quick taste—if it isn't sweet enough, add a tablespoon more sugar (this will very much depend on the sweetness of the wine and your personal preference). Remove the spices before serving.

64

GLÜHMOST – CIDRE CHAUD

Spiced apple cider for chilly autumn nights

Freshly pressed apple (and pear) juice can be found all over Switzerland in the fall. Although the fresh juice is particularly delicious, today much of the product is pasteurized, bottled, and available year-round.

Since at least the Middle Ages, farmers would make vinegar and lightly alcoholic drinks with their apple juice, which naturally ferments after a few days. It wasn't until the early 1900s that pasteurization (which stops the fermentation and allows it to remain alcohol-free) made it possible for the non-alcoholic version to be stored and sold at market.

You can use either alcoholic or non-alcoholic cider for this recipe—the non-alcoholic version is a great family-friendly alternative to mulled wine.

SERVINGS
4

INGREDIENTS

- 1 L (4 cups) apple juice or cider (alcoholic or not)
- 1 orange
- 1 lemon
- A pinkie-sized piece of ginger, peeled and cut in half
- 2 cloves
- 2 star anise
- 1 cinnamon stick
- ½ vanilla bean, sliced open

METHOD

- Fill a large pot with the apple juice or cider. With a vegetable peeler, peel off a few thin sections of orange and lemon rind (try to avoid the bitter white pith) and juice the fruit. Add this, plus the rest of the ingredients, to the pot, then warm over medium heat for about 20 minutes, being careful not to boil. Remove the spices before serving.

RESOURCES AND FURTHER READING

Here's where to look if you want to dive deeper into Swiss cooking:

The Culinary Heritage of Switzerland
The Kulinarisches Erbe der Schweiz/Patrimoine Culinaire Suisse/Patrimonio Culinario Svizzero is an astounding collection of information about traditional and historic Swiss food products. You can find it online in German, French and Italian.

Tiptopf/Croqu'menus/Cosa Bolle in Pentola?/Mintgin Cuschin
A common Swiss German expression of agreement and acceptance is "*Tip Top*." So what better name for the standard issue school cookbook than the pun: *Tiptopf* (*Topf* is German for pot). The French version is called *Croqu'menus*, and in Italian it's *Cosa Bolle in Pentola?* (which directly translates as "What Bubbles in the Pot?" but basically means "What's Cooking?"). A teacher in Laax, in the Romansch-speaking part of Switzerland, even made a version, called *Mintgin Cuschin*, in the fourth national language.

This book has been used in Swiss home economic classes since 1986. It provides information about processes and ingredients, and has many invaluable base recipes that can then be altered and adapted as needed. It's the most-purchased cookbook in the country and almost every household has a copy (we somehow have three). There's even a vegetarian version!

Betty Bossi
Created in 1956 to help sell margarine to the butter-friendly Swiss, the Betty Bossi brand has now grown to be one of Switzerland's dominant cooking authorities. You'll find her cookbooks in most Swiss households.

Aus Schweizer Küchen by Marianne Kaltenbach
You won't find a better collection of Swiss recipes and the customs that go along with them than this classic collection published by Hallwag in 1977.

My two favorite books about Swiss food in English are *A Taste of Switzerland* by Sue Style, published by Bergli Books in 1996, and the vintage classic *Tante Heidi's Swiss Kitchen* by Eva Maria Borer, published by Nicholas Kaye in 1965.

For a more detailed look at resources, plus a peek into my very large Swiss cookbook collection, have a look at my blog helvetickitchen.com.

ACKNOWLEDGMENTS

So many people have helped with this book—from taste testers and recipe testers to all the wonderful readers of my cookbook and blog. Thank you for providing feedback over the years!

It's always a delight to work with the team at Helvetiq—many thanks to Aude, Angela, Karin, and Ajša for your support on this project. And thank you to Heddi for your blessing on this project! It's always inspiring to talk Swiss food with you.

To my indefatigable recipe (and taste) testers Rosemarie, Jackie, Allana, Lyndsay, and Jane (and families!), thank you! And to my wonderful editors, Sam, Stuart, Mary, and Allana, thank you for helping me make sure I'm always saying what I mean.

A million thanks to Josy, Robi, Franziska, Vreni, Fabiana, Annina, and Richard for sharing recipes and sourcing books. And to my wonderful mom, who's always game to be a guinea pig, babysitter, chauffeur, or hand model.

Finally, thanks to Sam, who's the only one who can be trusted with *Zopf*-braiding in this house, and my bright little star, Stella—everything tastes better when you're helping in the kitchen or giggling at the table. Especially the soft cheese.

INDEX